Goldfish

Animal
Series editor: Jonathan Burt

Goldfish

Anna Marie Roos

REAKTION BOOKS

To Ian, again
To K

Published by

REAKTION BOOKS LTD
Unit 32, Waterside
44–48 Wharf Road
London N1 7UX, UK
www.reaktionbooks.co.uk

First published 2019
Copyright © Anna Marie Roos 2019

Printed and bound in China

A catalogue record for this book is available from the British Library

ISBN 978 1 78914 135 1

Contents

1 No Need to Carp: The Origins and Anatomy of a Goldfish

When people are asked what animal they would like to be if reincarnated, many respond 'a dolphin', those altruistic, smiling, social and sleek acrobats of the deep. But for me, it would be the humble goldfish, cared for by a winsome child who would call me 'Cheeto', 'Goldie' or 'Bubbles', and provide a reliable drift of fish flakes and a spacious aerated aquarium – 25 gallons of sheer tranquillity. As a bonus, I would get to be my favourite colour of orange and live in a Barbie-pink castle, appropriate environs for the oldest ornamental fish in the world.[1] Even Henri Matisse in his eightieth year claimed he 'wouldn't mind turning into a vermilion goldfish', the fish appearing in no less than nine of his paintings, for the artist a reminder of the sensuality and exoticism of Morocco.[2]

It would be a life prosaic yet glamorous, just like the goldfish itself, an animal that is at once ambiguous, liminal and surprising. Not for this creature does familiarity breed contempt. Rather, we should think of the goldfish as a 'human cultural artefact' created through a millennium of religious reverence and selective breeding for practical purposes, consumerist aims and aesthetic expression.[3] We will see in this book that goldfish are world travellers and shifting self-contradictions, at once rare and common, hero and villain, their relationships with humans often unpredictable.

Ryukin goldfish in an aquarium, produced from a mutation of the Japanese wakin goldfish.

The origins of the goldfish are ambiguous. Even when in the mid-eighteenth century Carl Linnaeus (1707–1778), the founder of binomial taxonomy, gave the goldfish its modern moniker – *Carassius auratus*, the golden carp – he was not describing the wild single-tailed progenitor, but an exotic twin-tailed individual.[4] Along with a captive raccoon and parrots that imitated Linnaeus's voice, croaking 'Blow your nose!', Linnaeus kept a number of goldfish in the botanical gardens of Uppsala University, trading information about fishy varieties with the Dutch naturalist Job Baster (1711–1775), who bred them in open-air ponds.[5] Although Baster offered Linnaeus some of his specimens, he worried about how to transport them alive to Sweden. Linnaeus instead received most of his goldfish from a former pupil, the physician Pehr af Bjerkén (1731–1744), who, while staying in London, was in contact with a breeder named Richard Guy, who had a pond at his country estate with fifty to sixty goldfish. Bjerkén brought them back by ship to Gothenburg, with Linnaeus writing in September 1759:

Illustration of the goldfish named *Cyprinus auratus* by Carl Linnaeus (now known as *Carassius auratus*), from Marc Bloch, *Ichtyologie* (1785–97).

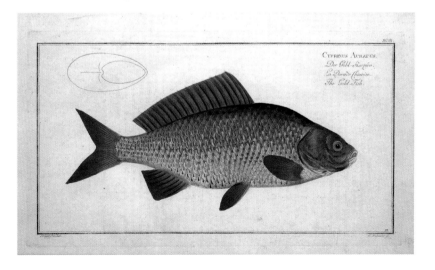

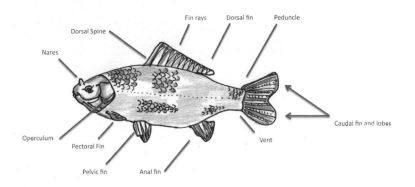

Fin rays Dorsal fin Peduncle

Dorsal Spine

Nares

Operculum

Pectoral Fin

Pelvic fin Anal fin

Vent

Caudal fin and lobes

Do please send the goldfish already tomorrow with a vessel to Uppsala; they do not freeze that easily; so I will be able to once again see them, something I have dreamed of all my days but never hoped. Let the skipper ask what price he wants, only I get them alive. God give I had them alive in my orangery.[6]

Anna Marie Roos, 'Goldfish Morphology', watercolour, pencil and ink on paper.

So by the eighteenth century, goldfish were almost everywhere, even in Sweden.

Part of their biogeographical success is that they are prolific breeders, pre-programmed to spawn when the weather turns warmer, the daylight lengthens and the water temperature gradually rises to 18–19°C (64–66°F). Males and females are fairly indistinguishable outside of mating season, but with the advent of spring, the females get rounder with a swollen abdomen, and the males sport little breeding tubercles, which look like white stars, covering their gills and pectoral fins. But the female is the

Bowl with Design of Fish, China, 1821–50, porcelain with coral-red and turquoise enamels.

real star of the show, sending out pheromones from her ovaries to let the male know it is time. The term 'pheromone' is derived from the Greek *pherein*, to transfer, and *hormon*, to excite, and what an exciting mating dance it is. Females also show a strong tendency to urinate when rising into spawning substrate (material where they release and lay their eggs, such as aquatic weeds), suggesting they might be using urine as an attractive lure.[7]

Because goldfish have no defined territories, the males fight each other to get close enough to fertilize a female's eggs or roe. Once the male 'has' his female, he pursues her relentlessly, nipping her fins and tail and chasing and nudging her stomach, to encourage her to release her eggs. The chase is a slow dance of attrition, until the female becomes so exhausted she cannot continue and releases her eggs, which are the size of a pinhead, and may be either somewhat transparent, yellowish or brilliant yellow. Breeders will often squeeze the females gently to get egg release at the optimum moment, and some inject a solution of dried carp pituitary or various synthetic hormone products to speed the final maturation and ovulation of eggs.[8] Not romantic, but effective.

As the goldfish is what is known as a 'portional spawner', releasing ova at each mating at eight- to ten-day intervals, the mating ritual can last for days. The female lays about 2,000 to 3,000 eggs, and the male then fertilizes the eggs by releasing milt, the goldfish equivalent of sperm. Because goldfish are messy breeders and spray eggs indiscriminately, the eggs are like little adhesive tapioca balls, sticking to grass and willow-like roots in the wild environment, or to spawning mops to simulate plants when in commercial breeding. Knitting yarn is ideal for making these mops, as the fibres catch the eggs, and the wool is soft on the fish's body, particularly when over-amorous males are chasing their quarry in and out of the strands.[9] Although the parents will eat some of the eggs for extra protein, the remaining fertilized eggs hatch after four to five days, with transparent fry of 3 to 8 mm (0.2–0.3 in.) long. Commercial breeders use methylene blue dye to stain the water so the fry can be better seen.

In highly bred varieties such as the telescope goldfish (also known as the demekin in Japan), the mating dance is even odder. The telescope goldfish's eyes project 2–5 cm (0.8–2 in.) from its head, making it very long-sighted and virtually blind underwater. Its very globular body makes swimming difficult for this unwieldy fish. The male in its pursuit will push the female with his head, turning and rolling her over and over like a ball for a distance of several metres, sometimes for a few days, until she evacuates all her ova.[10] It is the fish equivalent of rock and roll. The odd eyes are purely a genetic trait, not, as once was believed, produced by a course of treatment to young fish by 'straining them when

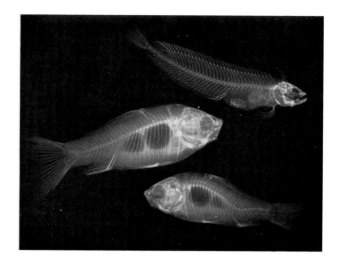

Josef Maria Eder (1855–1944) and Edward Valenta (1857–1937), goldfish skeletal anatomy, photogravure. Eder and Valenta published some of the first art photographs using the new discovery of X-rays by Wilhelm Conrad Röntgen, an experiment of the New Vision photographers in the 1910s and 1920s. This scientific and aesthetic image shows the elongated flexible armature of the goldfish body, with the swim bladders opaque in the image.

young in the desired angle in dark surroundings with a ray of light from one direction only'.[11]

But where did this fecund fish ultimately come from? This is a matter of current scientific debate and investigation. After all, Charles Darwin himself in his *Variation of Animals and Plants under Domestication* (1868) found it difficult to distinguish between variations and monstrosities. We know that the goldfish is native to China, the southern Amur River basin and Korea, and it was domesticated in China more than a thousand years ago.[12] Specifically, Chinese goldfish originate from southern China, from the lower Yangtze River.[13] Evidence based upon molecular genetics has suggested that in China, goldfish may have originated from hybridization of the red crucian carp and common carp, and during the evolutionary history of goldfish, the tail fin and body colour may have differentiated before other characteristics.[14] Over time, humans also eliminated lines of native goldfish that were aesthetically unappealing, leading to a decrease in genetic diversity of domesticated goldfish. The goldfish appears to be a product not only of selective breeding, but of molecular evolution and artificial selection working in tandem. As this book will show, each culture developed different strains of goldfish in accordance with aesthetic and cultural preferences, giving different perspectives of beauty.

In ancient China, the wild goldfish or *chi* (more correctly, *chi-yü*) was coloured dolphin grey or olive green with a deep body, its habitat in lateral waters or rivers and lakes. It was much bigger and less globular than our familiar pets, reaching an average size of 35 cm (14 in.) and a body mass of 1 kg (2 lb).[15] There were no teeth in the jaws, but a single line of teeth in the pharynx (throat) and, unlike common carp, it had no barbels or feeders at each corner of the mouth.

Chi are suction feeders, expanding their mouths to create a pressure difference, which causes water and food to flow in. When the mouth opens the gill openings are kept tightly closed. As George F. Hervey and Jack Hems describe: 'when the fish shuts its mouth, the pharynx is contracted, and the water is driven out through slits in the pharynx and over the gills. No water is swallowed because the gullet, situated behind the pharyngeal slits, is kept so tightly connected that no water can enter it and pass down' the digestive system.[16] This is how the fish prevents water from passing through the alimentary canal and why food particles do not escape through gill openings.

The more elongated shape of wild goldfish also meant they were steadier swimmers than many of the varieties cultivated today, as the swim bladders, which regulate buoyancy, have decreased in proportion to body size in domesticated goldfish. In fact, all the internal organs are compressed into a smaller area, which, if the bladder is malformed, or the fish become constipated and compress the swim bladder, leads them to swim upside down

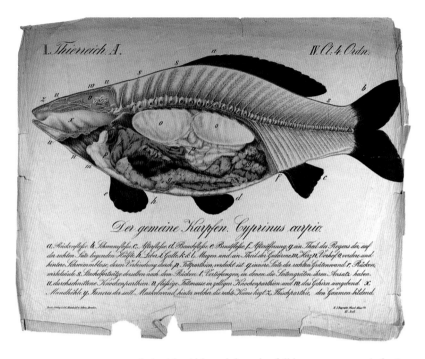

Cross-section from 1877 of a carp's internal organs. It is possible to see how deformities in the swim bladders (in the diagram 'O') can lead to digestive problems.

or on their side. Although breeder folklore recommends fasting the fish or feeding them peas to release the blockage, this has limited effectiveness. Much like pedigree dogs that have impaired gaits because of hip dysplasia resulting from selective breeding, the fancy fish suffers for its beauty. In fact, an eighteenth-century French work on goldfish (Edme-Louis Billardon de Sauvigny's *Histoire naturelle des dorades de la Chine*), based on a Chinese scroll portraying 92 different types, mistakenly classified a fish with air-bladder problems as the *shui-yü*, or the sleeper (*dormeur*). Sauvigny claimed it emerged as a variant in 1757 and was from Yangzhou, where breeders were apparently selling diseased or deformed fish as exotic varieties.

Goldfish normally sleep upright, and both wild and domesticated goldfish do not have eyelids so they sleep with their eyes open, becoming inactive and moving just enough to keep their stability. For these moving and unquiet spirits, it is eyes wide shut. That glassy-eyed stare from your pet fish may really be a glassy-eyed stare as they dream of food, water and sex, and of not being eaten themselves.

'Sleeper Fish', illustration from Edme-Louis Billardon de Sauvigny, *Histoire naturelle des dorades de la Chine* (1780).

Raw carp (sashimi) as medicine, from the Chinese *Materia Dietetica*, Ming dynasty (c. 1368–1644). The text, a dietetic herbal, instructs that fish *kuai* is any kind of fish cut into slivers. Crucian carp (*jiyu*) kuai is used to treat intestinal lumps, erysipelas (*dandu*), wind dizziness and so on. Kuai made with common carp (*liyu*) is used to treat cold Qi (breath or life spirit) consolidations in the heart and abdomen.

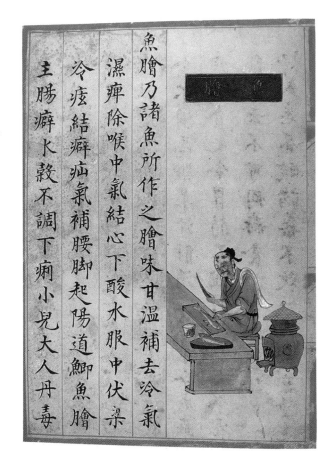

主腸癖水穀不調下痢小兒大人丹毒

冷痎結癖疝氣補腰脚起陽道鯽魚膽

濕痺除喉中氣結心下酸水服中伏梁

魚膽乃諸魚所作之膽味甘溫補去冷氣

膽

Though they do not blink, goldfish do 'speak'. Fish have dawn and dusk choruses just like birds, and even the humble goldfish produces a murmuring sound through its air bladder ducts connected to the oesophagus.[17] The sonic muscle, which is attached to the swim bladder, contracts and relaxes rapidly, making the bladder vibrate and producing a low-pitched drumming sound.

16

An article entitled 'Fish Noises' in *Life* magazine of 15 November 1943 described the rather technologically obsessed and playful efforts of Christopher Coates of the New York Aquarium. Dr Coates connected a hydroscope (waterproof microphone) to an oscilloscope, showing that excited fish emit rapid and louder sounds than calm fish, and some fish even purr like kittens. A feeding goldfish makes a steadier sound than an annoyed box-fish jabbed with a pencil. To set the article in some serious wartime context, it advised that the navy should 'take fish noises seriously', and 'train subchaser crews to distinguish them from the sound of a U-boat'. It is unlikely that the navy needed to worry too much about the hums of domesticated goldfish.

But the domesticated goldfish in ancient China had a right to be worried about being too conspicuous a target. Its wild cousin

Eyes wide shut: sleeping or staring?

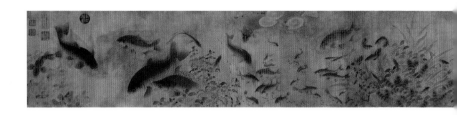

Liu Cai
(c. 1080–1120),
*Fish Swimming
amid Falling
Flowers*, handscroll,
ink and colour on
silk. This painting
of a pond of
mercy was by
a court painter
known for exact
representation
with fine-style
ink wash, down
to the 'very scales
of a fish's tail'.
Portraying fish
was thought
to be more
challenging
than other
animals because
their watery
habitat was a
barrier to direct
observation.

was a popular food in China, and there is speculation that fishing ponds could have been created in an early form of aquaculture. There were places like the Ninghai district where *chi* were served as food.[18] Cooked with salted ginger, they were considered a remedy for chronic dysentery.[19]

At some point in the distant past, gold and red fish appeared among the grey *chi* due to sudden genetic mutations. While *chi* are normally battleship- or silvery grey due to pigment-containing cells in their skin called melanophores, they do have a sprinkling of other pigment cells called erythrophores and xanthophores that produce red and yellow colours.[20] At some point, a rare mutation occurred that suppressed the grey pigment cells, producing shining red, golden and yellow *chi*. Because the goldfish also have a molecule (a nucleic acid) called guanine in their scales that makes them shiny, the golden fish shimmered as they swam.

Some ancient Chinese authors attached a supernatural significance to the strangely coloured fish, regarding them as sacred. The transformation must have seemed especially miraculous, as goldfish fry are grey or black, only becoming bedazzling as adults. There were reports of 'red fish' called *jīnyú* as far back as the Jin dynasty (AD 265–420) that swam in a lake near Mount Lu and in the Red River near Shaanxi.[21] In the work *Beauties of the Earth* written in 1239, we read that in the Lumao Pond of the Prefecture of Kiahsing, 'Governor Ting Ten-tsan of the T'ang dynasty [AD 618–907] found golden chi in his pond, which is the present West

18

Lake'.[22] As the Chinese word for fish (*yú*) is pronounced very similarly (but in a different tone) to the word for wealth, goldfish over time became symbols of prosperity, which may have accounted for their sacred status.

These goldfish were more conspicuous in clear waters and were easy prey, as anyone with a garden pond knows when a heron is on patrol. Buddhist monks fed and protected the fish in special ponds as religious practice to cultivate compassion and earn merit. It was also thought that eating these rare varieties could be dangerous; in AD 1223 it was reported that in the spring in

Detail of Liu Cai's *Fish Swimming.*

John Thomson, 'Sacred Fish-pond, Chinese temple', 1872, glass negative (scratched). Thomson produced a series of very early photographic images of his tour of China, including this pond of mercy.

Chi-cheng one could see gold and silver *chi* of 'the most delicious taste. But they are so mysterious that fishing boats approaching them often turn upside down'.[23]

The golden *chi* itself had a reputation for being a fussy eater, only shyly appearing when particular food was thrown. The love-lorn medieval poet Tu Tzu-Mei complained, 'Waiting by bridge for gold *chi* fair/ All day alone I loiter there'.[24] In the T'ang period, monks carved 81 such ponds of mercy near their temples to distil the Buddha's message: 'Reflected in the water the moon was pure illusion, empty form. There was nothing to discover but the nature of mind.'[25] In the twelfth century, Mei Tao-chen of the Song Dynasty wrote:

> Who knows the secret of massing wealth
> That he may build a pond broad as a brook?
> Where mercy shields the fish and turtle too
> And angler dare not tempt with baited hook?[26]

In modern Buddhism, goldfish are also actors in *fàng shēng* or 'mercy release', a practice that dates back to the third century. The ritual was traditionally governed by spontaneous acts of devotion, although modern 'mercy release' involves creatures being raised or caught primarily for sale to pious individuals to perform the act. Accompanied by the sound of robed Buddhist monks ringing bells and chanting sutras, in Taiwan alone 200 million wild animals each year are used in *fàng shēng* practice – not only goldfish, but monkeys, birds and baby turtles, the latter sold in markets for cooking or releasing.[27] As we will see later in this book, goldfish being released into the environment for religious purposes or just as unwanted pets have caused countless environmental catastrophes, leading government officials in America and Britain to ban the practice.[28] The goldfish's extreme hardiness and ability to breed prolifically overwhelms ecosystems and kills off other native species. So good for karma, but so bad for other fish. A sacred menace is the goldfish.[29]

Han Yu (768–824), a renowned T'ang dynasty Neo-Confucian scholar who considered Buddhism a foreign religion and mercy release a pernicious influence, was more prosaic about his delight with his own goldfish. He raised his fry in pottery basins half-buried in the ground, feeding them with tiny water fleas.[30] His writing about his delight with his ponds was an aesthetic expression of a golden age of Chinese literature in which he wrote poetry and developed the critical prose essay into a major literary form.[31] Han Yu asked:

Does the bowl
in the garden
mock nature
when night after night
green frogs gather

to prove it a pool?
Who says
you can't make a pond
out of a bowl?

By the Song dynasty, goldfish were domesticated in the pond of mercy at the emperor's Te Shou Palace in Hangzhou, now the capital of Zhejiang province in east China. Chao Kou, Prince of K'ang, later known as Emperor Kao-tsung (ruled 1127–62) had moved the palace south to Hangzhou due to the threat of northern Chin invaders. In 1162 the empress of the Song dynasty decreed for a special pond to be built and filled with *jīnyú*, forbidding those outside the imperial family from keeping goldfish of the yellow or xanthic variety.[32] As a common metaphor for the Song imperial family was a 'heavenly lake' versus the 'common stream', one wonders if the empress was trying to extend the metaphor with a heavenly fish kept out of the common waters.[33]

Emperor Kao-tsung had a reputation for extravagance and for being an animal lover. While his keeping of pigeons at the Imperial Palace was criticized, he was always a goldfish enthusiast. Perhaps the fish helped calm him as he spent much of his reign with his kingdom under threat, watching for years his two rival heirs, Po-ts'ung (Shen) and Po-chiu (Chü), in contention for power. By one account, Shen (the future Emperor Hsiao-tsung) was chosen due to his superior calligraphy, with another source claiming he was chosen because the serving maids assigned to him 'remained pure as jade'.[34] Whatever the reason, the emperor loved his goldfish, and the year before he died, he ordered the collection of silver and goldfish to restock his ponds.[35]

The collapse of the Song dynasty with the invasion of the Mongols and the advent of the Yuan dynasty meant records of goldfish cultivation became scarcer, though we know that

goldfish were brought to Beijing during this time. During the latter part of the Ming dynasty (1368–1644), however, there was a general transition from pools to earthenware and porcelain bowls, and the advent of more exotic breeds that could not survive in outdoor ponds.[36]

Captive and tamed, the fish could be cross-bred to produce for the first time the silver-white, golden-yellow, and black and tortoiseshell varieties, which were often given poetic names such as 'golden helmet' or 'brocaded back'.[37] Four important morphological characteristics – body shape, dorsal fin, eye shape and tail fin – began to be genetically modified to create variations and extraordinary traits. We see medieval Chinese reports of multiple-tailed fish, those with bulging eyes, and rare transparent fish where 'you can see both the stomach and intestine'.[38] These are now known as extreme manifestations of calico fish, the loss of an outer layer of pigment leaving the scales nearly transparent – perhaps a specimen for the aspiring medic?

A special breeding trade arose called *yu-er-huo* for rare varieties of goldfish and tortoises.[39] 'These breeders learned to feed the goldfish with a kind of red animalcule (*chi-hsia-er*) found in putrid water' to deepen their colours and 'discovered the secrets of propagating goldfish so as to enable them to offer a selection of rare varieties of goldfish to gods on festival days'.[40] In 1596, in *The Book of Vermilion Fish*, Chang Ch'ien-te noted, 'It is only in Wu [Soochow] that Vermilion Fish are at their best.'[41] Even today, commercial goldfish feeds often have colour enhancers like astaxanthin and carotenoids taken from spirulina (blue green algae) or crustaceans. Astaxanthin highlights red colour, which in some unfortunate cases turns white 'goldfish' pink. Goldfish can also turn pink by a form of blushing in response to emotions. The secretions of the fish itself, particularly its ductless glands, also affect the deepness of colour, and these secretions are associated with emotions. Fear results in paler colours, and excitement in deeper ones as the pigmentation expands.[42] The pH of water and the light affect the colour too. Hard water deepens black colours, as does light intensity in open ponds. An individual fish can be deep red or intense black in the summer, but if it is moved indoors with low-intensity light, it can turn orange or dark brown.[43]

By manipulation of the environment of the fish and selective breeding, a remarkable variety of colours in metallic goldfish has been produced. Although the Goldfish Society of America (GFSA) only recognizes two colour phases (orange-red and red and white), they have the most extensive listing and definition of goldfish colours among all the societies:

1. Ancient Bronze: brown to black with metallic shine
2. Black: coal black with no metallic shine
3. Blue scale: grey blue to sky blue
4. Chocolate: very dark brown
5. Copper: pale brown
6. Gold: orange
7. Green: olive green
8. Mahogany: reddish brown
9. Red: scarlet to oxblood
10. White: silvery white
11. Wild: light to dark greenish brown[44]

The Bristol Aquarists' Society also notes the differences in fin number and type between different varieties of fish. Individual fins in goldfish are composed of a double layer, which lie flush against each other forming a single fin that is two layers thick; several exotic varieties like the comet and shubunkin are all single-finned like their wild type ancestor.[45] By the Ming dynasty, we read of double-tailed fish, and varieties such as fantails and veil-tails, resulting when the fin layers split apart and grow separately from each other.[46] The *Hang-chou Fu Chih* (*c.* 1600) noted, 'There are those with three tails, five tails, even as many as seven tails . . . these are all what have been produced by fanciers in recent times'.[47] Some even appeared without a dorsal fin.

Multiple tails is perhaps the most remarkable feature developed in goldfish evolution.[48] This is because in fin development there are associated bony structures embedded in the muscles that are attached to the fin rays, so duplication of caudal and anal fins is accompanied by duplication of the bony structures. Sometimes in embryonic development, the anal fin fails to develop at all because the underlying bony structure was inhibited genetically. This makes breeding multiple-tailed fish unpredictable, as the

Stem cup,
1426–36,
Jingdezhen
porcelain.

breeder will not only not know if a single or double fin will develop, but if 'any fin develops at all'.[49] As a result, there is a dizzying array of varieties. As the Bristol Aquarists' Society indicates:

> There are long-bodied twintail types with the caudal fin completely divided, for example the jikin (or peacock tail) and the wakin, and long-bodied tri-tail types in which only the lower lobe is divided; these are less familiar to us in the West than the short-bodied twintails. Then there are the short-bodied, long-finned twintails, which were developed from a short-finned twintail precursor . . . veiltails, orandas, globe eyes and the broadtail moor.[50]

With an exotic fish, one could procure an exotic bowl. Emperor Hong Wu founded a porcelain factory in 1369 that produced 'large tubs, decorated with images of dragons and clouds, for fish and aquatic plants'.[51] In the Ming dynasty in the reign of the Wanli Emperor, it was written that 'there was nothing that could not be made of porcelain', as porcelain artistry became a monopoly of Jingdezhen in the province of Jiangxi.[52] The kilns of Jingdezhen (Ching-te Chen) became a global manufacturing and distribution centre for ceramic wares. The ceramic archives from the Imperial Court of 1554 revealed that along with 26,350 bowls with 30,500 matching saucers, 6,000 ewers and 6,900 wine cups were commissioned from the potteries.[53] The porcelain stem cup opposite, circa 1426–36, from Jingdezhen, is decorated with goldfish underglazed red. The fish are painted in copper oxide, a material very difficult to control during firing, adding to the preciousness of the piece.[54]

There were also factory orders for 680 large garden fishbowls, costing forty taels each, a small fortune. These first Ming goldfish bowls of porcelain at first glance seem straightforward in their decorations of aquatic scenes of golden fish, water plants and lotus flowers. But these illustrations were a visual-verbal pun in the Chinese language:

金魚滿塘
jin yu man tang
a pond full of gold fish

金玉滿堂
jin yu man tang
a hall filled with
gold and jade[55]

The phrase was pronounced similarly, yet had different characters, so the bowl was therefore a painted wish that one's hall or home be full of gold and jade or wealth.

Jin yu man tang is also a common phrase wishing prosperity in the Chinese Lunar New Year, and many families even now purchase goldfish for display during this period. The art of *feng shui* or geomancy advocates the keeping of nine *chi* (eight red and one black) to bring good luck to the owner, and Chinese and

Yashima Gakutei, *Red Carp Ascending a Waterfall*, c. 1820s, woodblock print, ink and colour on paper. The carp leaping the Dragon Gate in the waterfall was a common theme in Japanese art, as well as Chinese.

Singaporean lottery tickets are sold in red envelopes or *hóngbāo* with goldfish designs.

Goldfish bowls could also be inscribed with the symbol *li* 鯉 or carp; it had the same sound as *li* 利, which means monetary gain. The carp was also a special symbol for scholars, as it was believed to swim upriver to the Dragon Gate, leap it and become a dragon. This obstacle course was a symbol of the Byzantine hoops the scholar had to jump through to pass imperial examinations overseen by the Board of Rites (*libu*) and become a government official. These exams were meritocratic, allowing a peasant child to become a government official, but the pass rate was less than 5 per cent. The incredible amount of scholarly energy and rote learning required for the exams was often channelled into prose and poetry when aspiring scholar-officials failed to obtain their degrees, so it is not surprising that the *li* even found its way onto porcelain.[56] One can imagine a successful student lucky and wealthy enough to receive one treasuring their fishbowl.

This Ming goldfish bowl has its interior decorated with aquatic plants, and its base has a six-character reign mark *Daming Jiajing nien zhi*, meaning 'made in the reign of Jiajing (1522–66) of the Great Ming'. We usually think of Ming porcelain as blue-and-white ware, the blue colour from the firing of cobalt oxide, the

Goldfish bowl from the Ming dynasty, Jiajing period (1522–66), Jingdezhen, Jiangxi province, South China porcelain (Wucai ware).

whiteness from the addition of kaolin to the glaze. Most export porcelain in the seventeenth and eighteenth centuries was in this popular colour scheme. But colours for Imperial Court porcelain were subject not only to the possibilities of technology, but to the 'requirements of ritual' and the 'aspirations of taste'.[57] The emperor as the Son of Heaven was charged with maintaining universal harmony, which was defined in part by element, number, season and colour.

CHINESE CONCEPTION OF COLOUR: MING (1368–1644) AND
QING (1644–1911) PORCELAIN

ELEMENT	PROPERTY	COLOUR	DIRECTION	SEASON	NUMBER (FENG SHUI)
Wood	cold	green	east	spring	8
Fire	warmth	red	south	summer	7
Earth	humidity	yellow	centre	72 days	5
Metal	dryness	white	west	autumn	9
Water	coolness	black	north	winter	6

Table One, from Louise A. Cort and Jan Stewart, *Joined Colours: Decoration and Meaning in Chinese Porcelain* (Washington, DC, 1993). Each season was 72 days long, and eighteen days were subtracted from the other four seasons and set aside for the Earth King.

Imperial porcelain thus was subject to formulated regulations that considered season, setting, rank and occasion. Members of the imperial family were allowed a prescribed combination of two or more colours, with diversity of colour increasing as rank increased. As mentioned above, because red painted in copper oxide is very difficult to control during firing, there are far fewer porcelain bowls painted in red than in blue; polychromed and exquisite porcelain was extremely prized. Bowl shapes were developed from 1700 from half-barrels to 'hemispherical shapes with rounded sides at the top', looking more like modern fishbowls.[58]

The goldfish could appear on other forms of porcelain such as wine jars. Designs of golden fish and the associations with both good fortune and fertility suggest that jars like these were created for young, affluent couples to celebrate their marriage.

The creation of the goldfish bowl in the Ming dynasty saw a gradual shift in ownership of the prized fish from the wealthy elite or institutions such as temples or monasteries to more ordinary connoisseurs. Once there was common private ownership, the goldfish really went on a global swim.

Goldfish were introduced to Japan in the sixteenth century and from Japan exported to Europe: Portugal in 1611, England in 1711 and France in 1755. From thenceforward, goldfish were introduced throughout Europe and most of the world, reaching the United States by the nineteenth century.[59] As we will see in the next chapter, this small fish swam in a big pond.

2 The Japanese Goldfish

In the early seventeenth century, goldfish were imported indirectly from China to Japan, specifically to Sakai, near Osaka. During the Edo period, Japan's government closed the country off to the world, preventing migration and trade from anyone but the Dutch, so Dutch ships would bring in Chinese goods. It is said that a Dutch schooner brought the fish, which a samurai, a retainer in the service of the Koriyama clan, bought at a high price, devoting himself to their care. In 1724, Lord Yanagisawa brought goldfish when his fief was transferred from Kai to Yamatokōgri-yama (Nara Prefecture), and encouraged goldfish breeding among the samurai class. From here the Japanese goldfish was born. Engelbert Kaempfer (1651–1716), a surgeon and botanist of the Dutch East India Company who worked in Japan from 1690 to 1692, noted:

> in China and Japan, and almost all over the Indies, this fish is kept in ponds, and fed with flies before their wings come out . . . in some small houses and Inns of less note, where there is not room enough, neither for a garden, nor trees, they have at least an opening or window to let the light fall into the back rooms, before which, for the amusement and diversion of travellers, is put a small tub, full of water, wherein they commonly keep some gold or silver

fish, as they call them, being fish with gold or silver-colour'd tails alive.[1]

His observations were hard won. The shogunate of Japan did not want any information on Japan to reach foreigners (for example, it was strictly forbidden to sketch any government or military building). Kaempfer cleverly made drawings to which he added descriptions in Arabic and was able to get them out of the country, publishing his observations posthumously in *The History of Japan* in 1727.[2]

Goldfish keeping was reserved for samurai and aristocracy. The keeping of goldfish (*kingyo*) as pets only became popular among the general public in the later Meiji period (1868–1912), after the Edo military government ended, marking the end of the feudal regime and the cessation of the government of the shogun. The samurai's power disappeared, along with their livelihood. In compensation, samurai were given five to seven and a half years of stipend income in the form of interest-bearing bonds, so they could buy plots of government land at a discounted price or begin their own business, such as goldfish rearing.[3] This was part of a samurai rehabilitation programme (*shizoku jusan*) to find them useful employment, and having had little training other than that of a warrior, many turned what had been a pastime into a livelihood.[4] Goldfish cultivation became a 'side job for clansmen and samurai . . . and gradually developed into a thriving side business for jobless samurai'.[5]

With the ending of feudalism, people were free to choose their occupation and move without restrictions. By providing a new environment of political and financial security and investing in communication and transportation infrastructure, the government made possible investment in new industries and technologies. This gradually led to more disposable income in

Sō Shizan, *Flowers and Goldfish*, 18th century, hanging scroll, ink and colour on silk. As we will see, when the Japanese begin keeping goldfish, they have their own interpretation of the goldfish bowl.

An illustration of a Japanese goldfish vendor, for a hobbyist plastic model kit of a goldfish stall.

Japan, and by the early nineteenth century goldfish had become affordable for ordinary Japanese citizens. 'Every summer, they were a popular commodity because, psychologically at least, viewing fish swimming in delicate glass bowls tempered the heat.'[6] Goldfish vendors carried their wares in wooden tubs suspended from a wooden bar, moving through crowds on fête days, and even now there is always a person to provide hollow balls of coloured rice flour to be thrown into the many goldfish ponds that dot the cityscapes. The balls are light and float like corks as the fish push them around in their efforts to eat them, and as they become soaked they disintegrate and sink, and are finally devoured.[7]

Koriyama in the Fukushima Prefecture in northeast Japan is still a centre of goldfish breeding today, and the home of the

Koriyama Goldfish Museum housed in the Yamato Kingyoen building, with a large goldfish painted on the side. Along with assorted goldfish memorabilia, including two pickled goldfish that belonged to the Japanese emperor in the nineteenth century, there are fifty shallow concrete ponds housing with an area of 14,000 square metres (150,000 sq. ft) in which rare goldfish swim; the annual production sometimes exceeds 600,000 fish.[8] The shops in the area sell a variety of goldfish and goldfish toys aimed not only at the serious collector, but at children.

The tradition of goldfish as pets for children is fairly ancient, mentioned by Luís Fróis in 1585, a Jesuit missionary in Japan who wrote one of the earliest comparisons of Western and Japanese cultures. Although the early modern Japanese did not celebrate children's birthdays, they did have festivals on 'Girls' Day' and 'Boys' Day', visiting local shrines where there were booths selling goldfish in glass bottles, tiny kinetic toys, toys that made soap bubbles (*shabou*), or games like *kingyo sukui* or 'goldfish scooping'.[9]

In the Edo period (1615–1868) there was an increased interest in children's lives, evidenced by several woodblock prints that resulted in the emergence of a genre of prints known as *kodomo-e* (literally, 'children pictures'). These images of children at play, and images of children with their mothers (*oyako-e*), often feature goldfish as children's amusements. Kitagawa Utamaro (d. 1806), best known for his prints of beautiful women, was one of a number of important print designers of the Edo period of *kodomo-e*. In these examples, young children are mischievously teasing rare goldfish in their porcelain bowl, and a young woman holds up a goldfish in a glass bottle while another is scooping the fish.

By the nineteenth century, the Western-style aquarium had come to Japan, but the portrayals of women were remarkably similar to *kodomo-e*, as we can see in the 1913 print of 'Goldfish' by Takeuchi Keishū. This work is a *kuchi-e*, literally a 'mouth

Japanese goldfish cultivation pools.

Totoya Hokkei (1780–1850), *Gold-fish in a Glass Bottle*, polychrome woodblock print (Surimono).

Kitagawa Utamaro, *Kingyo: Scenes from Everyday Life*, c. 1793–1804, woodblock print. You can see the goldfish scoop by the bowl, also decorated with goldfish.

picture', or introduction that told a story. *Kuchi-e* were handmade woodblock prints that served as a printed frontispieces for Japanese literary and romance magazines that were published at the turn of the twentieth century, such as *Bungei Kurabu*. The pieces were designed to illustrate the magazine story, and most subjects were of *bijin-ga*, images of beautiful women, but many give us an inside view into Japanese domestic life at the turn of the twentieth century. Very fine artists such as Keishū made them because they were a source of reliable income. When his son mentioned his desire to become an artist, Keishū replied, 'If you are

Takeuchi Keishū,
Goldfish, Kuchi-e,
1913, woodblock
print, ink and
colour on paper.

Kawanabe Kyōsai,
*Two Children
Playing with
Goldfish*, c. 1887,
album leaf, ink and
colour on silk.

able to live on air and water, you may become an artist.'[10] Almost
as the goldfish he portrayed.

Some images show the game of *kingyo sukui*, or goldfish scooping, a common sight at Japanese summer street festivals (*matsuri*),
and at the 'national scooping contest' in Yamatokōriyama (Nara
Prefecture) held annually on the third Saturday and Sunday in

August. Yamatokōriyama is another national site of goldfish breeding due to its favourable water supply, having nearly sixty goldfish farms over 90 hectares (222 ac). Goldfish cultivation there dates to 1724, when it was sponsored by Lord Yanagisawa Yoshisato.[11]

In 2007 the thirteenth *kingyo sukui* championship was held, with 1,116 participants, and in 2011 the team title was awarded to three players who scooped 173 goldfish.[12] *Kingyo sukui* started in the late Edo period, about 1810. It is a version of the fairground amusement where you manoeuvre a metal claw to grab stuffed toys, releasing them into a chute and conveying them to the person waiting outside the glass enclosure, except the toys are live fish. It is annoyingly impossible, an unfair funfair, or in Japanese: *kodomo-damashi* (cheating the kids).

In the Japanese scooping game, there is a large tank of goldfish, and a several scooping nets (called *poi*) made of thin gauze or paper, which break easily. The punter attempts to catch the goldfish before the *poi* falls apart or breaks. Each try is about 500 yen (U.S.$4.39), and operators will often give away a goldfish if a contestant is summarily unsuccessful. There are also different strengths of paper or gauze: no. 4 (young kids), no. 5 (beginner), no. 6 (standard), no. 7 (expert), and if the game is played at a children's party, rubber or plastic fish are used, sometimes with hinged tails to 'swim' more realistically. Goldfish-scooping expert Koji Shimomura is more sanguine and advises, 'You need to level the *poi* underwater and scoop the goldfish from the head.' He now runs a training school outside his flower shop in Yamatokōriyama. He has taught over four hundred people 'how to scoop', imparting to the young sportsmanship, politeness and care for the fish.[13]

Goldfish scooping is such a beloved part of Japanese culture that artist Riusuke Fukahori recreates exquisitely rendered representations of scooping ponds by painting the fish in acrylic and covering the paintings in successive layers of resin to represent

Goldfish lantern festival (Yanai city, Yamaguchi Prefecture). These lanterns are traditionally flown to celebrate 13 August, Obon, a holiday of the ancestors.

water, giving a three-dimensional effect. In one piece, a metal gold-fish scoop is even embedded into the 'pond' with painted goldfish 'swimming' in and out of the scoop, the ultimate goldfish optical illusion. All the artist does is paint goldfish, and he claims the fish is his muse.[14] After all, in a Japanese twist of grammar, *kingyo sukui* (金魚すくい) 'can also be read 金魚救い – goldfish salvation'.[15]

In 2006 the Japanese game company Namco even launched a video game version of *kingyo sukui* (Japan release only), one of nine mini-games in its *Ennichi no Tatsujin*, or *Festival Master*. It was Namco's first game using the Nintendo Wii console. It simulates the experience of playing the game at a Japanese carnival with a virtual Wiimote *poi*, its advertising trailer showing a frenetic synchronized dance with the console set to the beat of Japanese festival drums. Another of the games is called *Takoyaki*, or fried octopus, a favourite festival treat. The Wiimote replicates a metal

Goldfish scooping.

Goldfish scooping, Hyōgo, 2014.

pick used to stop the octopus balls from burning. Needless to say, *Festival Master* did poorly in reviews and sales.

Goldfish have become ubiquitous in Japanese culture. Sometimes the cultural referents are exquisite. Goldfish in water appear on lacquered *inrō* cases (small purses to hang on the obi or sash, as kimonos do not have pockets) and kimonos themselves, sometimes resist-dyed and painted on silk gauze (*ro*) or subtly patterned in the weave. Goldfish as fertility symbols were patterns for robes for the Buddhist ceremony of *jūsan-mairi* (literally, 'thirteenth temple visit'), where girls receive a blessing as they become women. This particular summer robe with its carp, morning glories and lilies was woven with fantail goldfish and dated from 1876. It was worn on a pilgrimage to Arashiyama Hōrinji, a temple in Saga Kyoto. The young lady crossed a bridge to the temple with its spectacular views, but the tradition was that after she received her blessings to enter adulthood, she could not look back, a temptation indeed for the wearer of this goldfish kimono.

Sometimes the cultural referents mediate between sacred and profane. Old phone booths in Japan have been converted into goldfish aquariums for public delight, demonstrating the multi-species character of urban space and relationships within it. The

Case (*inrō*) with design of goldfish and reed with wave pattern, *c.* 18th–19th century, lacquer, roiro, red and gold *hiramakie*. The *inrō* was a traditional Japanese case for holding small objects, which was suspended from the obi or sash of the kimono, as the robe lacked pockets. The netsuke was a toggle that helped suspend the *inrō*. Some cases were purely utilitarian, but some, as in this example, were examples of very fine craftsmanship.

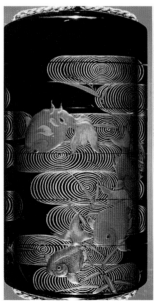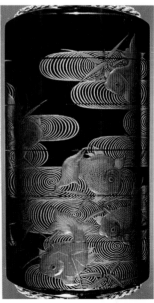

Unlined summer kimono (*Hito-e*) with carp, water lilies and morning glories, *c.* 1876.

artist collective who made the tanks, complete with aerating bubblers and old payphones intact, is known appropriately as Kingyobu: the 'Goldfish Club'. These are the modern Buddhist ponds of mercy, saving the fish and the phone booths from landfill.

But the telephone booth aquaria are temporary, ephemeral, much like the creations of Japanese designer Daisuke Akiyama. She has created goldfish bubble wrap, giving the rather magical illusion of tiny goldfish swimming in each bubble. 'We usually have an inclination to pop bubble wrap,' says Akiyama. 'But by printing

Japanese lionhead oranda toy. The toy fish rolls along and the fins move as it swims across the tabletop.

goldfish I've made it psychologically more difficult to pop.'[16] And more difficult to throw away or consider a funfair prize.

The Japanese goldfish is not always associated with ephemeral art and beauty, however, but with disposable consumer culture and with waste, natural or artificial. Goldfish can decorate the tacky – plastic toys, ashtrays and key rings. There is even a term, *kingyo no fun*, literally 'goldfish crap', a phrase that dates from the Edo period and idiomatically means a sycophant or hanger-on, like the excrement that follows the fish around. Kenji Miyazawa (1896–1933), the Japanese poet and children's author, wrote:

> *Yūmei-jin no mawari ni wa, uzō-muzō no hitotachi ga kingyo no fun no yō ni tsuite kuru mono da.*
> (Famous people attract all kinds of goldfish droppings like flies.)

A 'goldfish poop' or toady gang is a set of video game characters that have to be fought numerous times, devolving from threats to pesky nuisances.[17] *Kingyo no fun* is also the name of a series of manga comic books by Hina Sakurada about a tortured relationship

Ohara Shōson, *Pair of Goldfish (Kingyo)*, 1926, colour woodblock print.

Shang Zhaoshan and Juqu Shannong, *Jin yu tu pu* or *Illustrated Album of Goldfish*, 1848, National Library of China. This is the earliest existing Chinese work with colour illustrations about goldfish. Note the brilliant colour and lifelike pose.

此類品佳
但脊有鬐
者名草種
以無鬣者
為工二種
原譜所無
今隨在有
之故附入

between an adolescent girl named Kingyo and her cousin Kiku-Chan who has an inappropriate crush on her. In this case, Kiku-Chan is the hanger on.

The Japanese goldfish trade has been in decline since the 1970s, especially around the city of Yatomi, Aichi Prefecture, owing to the strength of the yen, water pollution due to urbanization, and to diverging recreational interests (including the playing of video games). At the height of the industry in 1960, the Fisheries Cooperative Association was launched for farmers, wholesalers and shop owners from around Yatomi, including the Tobishima district and the cities of Tsushima and Aisai.[18] In the 1970s, there were 320 members, but in 2011, only 119 remained. One reason is that because farmers must constantly monitor fish health and water temperature, they are tied to their farms, and the younger generation opted for careers in metropolitan Nagoya. Despite these setbacks, the Japanese are still some of the leading breeders of goldfish. Koriyama still sells about 70 million goldfish a year.

The Japanese goldfish is a very different creature from its Chinese predecessor. In contrast to the familiar pets in the West, in Japan goldfish are bred predominantly for appreciation from the top view only, which in turn has influenced traits in selective breeding as well as designs of bowls and ponds. Chinese goldfish fanciers over time preferred extraordinary traits resulting in exotic varieties and large breeding facilities. In the first International Goldfish Championships held in China in Fuzhou in 2012, one award winner was a 1.75-kg (3-lb 5-oz) prized specimen fish, bred for sheer size. Japanese goldfish however are conceived more as dynamic works of art, their composure and swimming balance more important than colouration, which is of prime importance in China.

Japanese connoisseurs have focused on perfecting features in extant breeds, creating four main varieties: wakin (common

Japanese goldfish), ranchu (maruko or round fish), ryukin (loocho goldfish) and the demekin or shina kin (goggle-eyed).[19] Watonai (newly found variety), shukin (autumn brocade), shubunkin (vermilion variegated goldfish), oranda shishigashira (rare lion-headed) and kinranshi (brocaded goldfish) are other popular varieties resulting from the crossbreeding of the initial four. The shubunkin, for instance, are produced from cross-breeding a wakin with a single tail fin and a calico telescope. The fish has a mix of nacreous scales and normal scales, coming in a variety of colours and patterns, mixing red, black and sky blue.

Although the syllable 'wa' is included in the name of the fish, indicating Japanese origins, the wakin were actually the first gold-fish imported into Japan from China in the early seventeenth century.[20] They have small heads, long bodies and short tail and fins, and usually are brightly coloured (usually bright red, red-and-white or white). They are generally the hardiest, largest, cheapest in price and resemble the carp: 'white fish with dark red spots and symmetrical three- or four-lobe tail fins are very valuable'.[21]

In contrast to the common wakin, the Japanese ranchu (Katakana or maruko or round fish), derived from repeated breeding of wakin, are some of the most iconic and expensive goldfish. Although the first ranchu bred did not have headgrowths, most varieties now do, developing a warty growth in its second year (a largely harmless enlargement of the fish's normal papillae in the skin of the head). When the headgrowth covers equal portions of the crown, the area below the eyes and the gills, it is called the lionhead, or the oranda shishigashira.

The oranda combines the hooded growth of the ranchu with the flowing causal tail fins of the ryukin, which fans out when it stops swimming. The Chinese refer to the oranda as the 'flower

Diagram of types of Japanese fish, from Hugh M. Smith, *Japanese Goldfish* (1909).

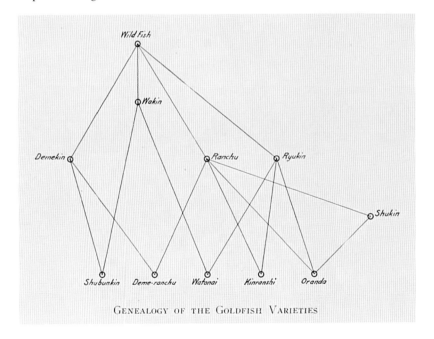

GENEALOGY OF THE GOLDFISH VARIETIES

Yamada Masanao, netsuke of *c.* 19th century, wood with inlaid eyes of horn. This ugly and adorable goldfish is the 'lion-head goldfish' or oranda, highly regarded and bred in Japan.

of the water'. A very popular variety is a redcap oranda, and a blue variety has been recently developed.[22]

If the growth on the ranchu is on the crown, it is called the *tokin*, after a priest's helmet-shaped hat. If the growth on the gill covers is most predominant, it is called the *okame*, named after Japanese folk masks of chubby-cheeked old women, which are mainly connected with religious drama, especially Shinto kagura festivals.[23]

Although the 1747 publication *Kingyo yōsan-sō* (Book on Caring for Goldfish) referred to the ranchu fish as the 'Korean goldfish', the name 'ranchu' means 'Holland worm', named at a time when anything that Dutch traders brought to the Japanese was deemed strange or noteworthy. The Spanish and Portuguese traded with Japan, but they were ultimately expelled which meant that throughout most of the early modern era, as we have seen, the Netherlands was the only Western power allowed to exchange goods with the Japanese. The Vereenigde Oost-Indische Compagnie (Dutch East India Company), or voc, administered the trade relationship. From

1641, the VOC was assigned the island of Deshima (Nagasaki), which was connected to the mainland by a bridge. Members of the VOC could not leave the island without a Japanese escort, and were limited to visits to the Shoguns Court in Edo to show their allegiance:

The Dutch delegation consisted of the chief, the highest-ranking merchant, other company staff, a surgeon, litter bearers, interpreters, horses and luggage. The whole trip took about three months, of which two to three weeks were spent in Edo. In total, the party travelled a distance in excess of 2,000 kilometres. On arrival at the Shogun's palace, the chief had to wait for ages before being allowed to appear in the 'hall of the hundred mats'. The Shogun remained invisible behind a screen, never addressing his visitor directly. The chief would present the gifts and throw himself to the ground in homage to the Shogun.

Shinnosuke Matsubara, *The Shubunkin*, 1909. The shubunkin are produced from cross-breeding a wakin with a single tail fin and a calico telescope. The fish has a mix of nacreous scales and normal scales, coming in a variety of colours and patterns, mixing red, black and sky blue.

THE SHUBUNKIN
SPECKLED GOLDFISH
NATURAL SIZE

COPYRIGHT, 1909, BY S. MATSUBARA

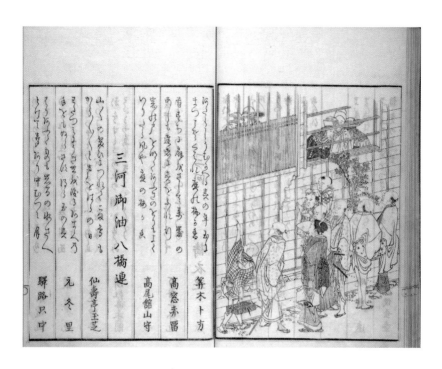

Katsushika Hokusai, 'Curious Japanese Watching Dutchmen', c. 1802, woodblock-printed book, ink on paper.

Once the gifts had been handed over to the Shogun, the daimyo, Japanese liege lords in the Shogun's entourage, also received presents. At the end of the visit, the Dutch received a traditional present: thirty silk kimonos, so-called imperial coats.[24]

The shogun demanded not only textiles from India and China, spices like saffron, scientific instruments (magnets, compasses and quadrants) and books, but various animals including cockatoos, an ostrich and horses.[25] The exotic nature of these creatures would make any odd goldfish like the ranchu, even one that was Japanese bred, seem 'Dutch' to the Edo people.

The ranchu, the compact 'king of goldfish', are preferably viewed from above, exhibited in shallow bowls and divided by age: *tosai* (fish born this year), *nisai* (fish born last year) and *oya* (more than two years old) which reach up to 4 sun (14 cm/5.5 in.) in length. The Japanese enjoy seeing the distinctive traits of the fish mature over time, comparing them to sumo wrestlers who become more proficient as they develop as athletes. The ranchu fish, like the sumo wrestler, is rounded, imposing, a representation of balance, proportion, graceful movement and power. The best shaped are those which are elongated and oval, like a koban, or Japanese coin. Ranchu of uniformly bright red were traditionally the most prized, although as with koi, the colour on a ranchu

Japanese ranchu goldfish.

can change as it matures. With age, they often become whiter, and in 2004 a 98 per cent white fish won the All Japan Show; yellow heads are also in current favour.[26]

The name 'ryukin' derives from Ryukyu, the Japanese name for the Chinese Luiku, the islands lying between Taiwan and the Japanese mainland. Although the fish originated in China, it arrived in the Kagoshima Prefecture in Kyūshū, and it is also known as the onaga or 'long-tail' and the 'nagasaki' after the city in northern Kyūshū.[27] As Hugh Smith states in his work on Japanese goldfish varieties:

> The characteristic features of this variety are the greatly shortened body, the rounded and bulging abdomen, and the long, flowing fins. The back is elevated, the head rather pointed in profile but broad when viewed from above . . . and the shortening of the body in its long axis, results in strong curvature of the spine. The particular point to which

Genroku-koban coin, 1696–1710.

this variety is bred, deformity; but this is amply compen-
sated for by the beauty of fins and colors.[28]

Ryukins tend to be smaller (not exceeding 19–20 cm/7.5–8 in.),
with an extended abdomen, and usually are variegate with vermilion mottled with white. 'Such a fish, with its long, flowing,
graceful fins, slowly swimming in quiet dignity, has been likened
. . . to the Japanese court ladies . . . dressed in long robes and
walking with sedate grace and dignity.'[29]

Some of the oddest goldfish to come out of Japan are the
chōtengan (upward-looking eyes) or celestial fish, also known as
the deme ranchu. It is a mutation of the telescope fish, and anecdotally was said to have resulted from being raised in jars for so
many generations, forcing it to look up.[30] This breed, along with
the *suihōgan* or bubble-eye with its large pouch-shaped eyes (also
known as the hamato or 'frog head'), was imported from China

61

Bubble-eyed
goldfish or
suihōgan.

in the 1950s and further developed in Japan. The fluid-filled sacs around the eyes wobble as the *suihōgan* fish swims, and it has a longer body than the ranchu. Symmetrical eyes are most prized, and connoisseurs of these fish have to be sure there are no sharp objects in the aquarium.

3 The English and European Goldfish, 1500–1800

Despite these Japanese innovations, the first goldfish to come to Europe was not via secluded Japan, but via Macao (across the Pearl River Delta from Hong Kong) and Portuguese traders who established a port there in 1557.[1] It seems that by the seventeenth century, goldfish may have reached England. On 28 May 1665, Samuel Pepys wrote in his diary, 'Thence home and to see my Lady Pen [Lady Margaret Penn].' She was described by Pepys the year previously as a 'well-looked, fat, short, old Dutchwoman, but one that hath been heretofore pretty handsome, and is now very discreet, and, I believe, hath more wit than her husband.' Pepys reported during his May visit 'at her home' that he and his wife 'were shown a fine rarity: of fishes kept in a glass of water, that will live so for ever; and finely marked they are, being foreign'.[2] Historian Caroline Grigson has cautioned that as they were 'finely marked' they possibly could have been Chinese paradise fish from Southeast Asia instead of goldfish.[3]

We do know for certain, however, that in 1711, the collector, botanist and entomologist James Petiver (c. 1665–1718) recorded in the second volume of his *Gazophylacium naturae et artis* that he possessed 'China Silver-tail' and 'China gold-tail' fish 'brought hence alive' (a 'gazophylacium' is a treasury or offertory).[4] According to John Henry Gray, the nineteenth-century archdeacon of Hong Kong, 'silver-fish are of greater value [in China] than gold-fish, a circumstance which is probably due to their comparative rarity', so Petiver had a precious fish.[5] Petiver also included two drawings of them in his 'Gazophylactik Tables', which featured figures of 610 other plants and animals drawn after dried and live specimens. In hopes of patronage, Petiver dedicated each of his tables to an august figure, in this case Jacob Bobart, the botany professor of Oxford.[6]

Petiver, with the assured patronage of Sir Hans Sloane (founder of the British Museum), became apothecary to the Charterhouse in 1700, establishing an independent shop at White Cross Street, Aldersgate. Petiver's interest in animals and plants was no doubt tied with his expertise in materia medica; a genus of plants, *Petiveria*, is named in his honour. As D. E. Allen stated, 'By as early as 1690 Petiver's reputation was such that he was in frequent correspondence with the country's leading naturalists and a member of a circle of fellow enthusiasts who met informally in and around London.'[7] The botanist John Ray (1627–1705) thought Petiver 'a man of greater correspondence in Africa, India, and America than any one I know of besides'.[8] Recent scholarship has revealed, for example, that Petiver had a long exchange of letters with the Catalan botanist Joan Salvador.[9] He was also an inveterate collector. According to Allen, 'By 1697 Petiver's herbarium alone amounted, on his own reckoning, to between 5,000 and 6,000 specimens, and he was ready to start reaping some scientific acclaim for the huge investment of time and effort by describing in print some of the contents of the by then famous Museum Petiverianum.'[10] On Petiver's death, Sloane bought his library and collection for £4,000; some two hundred volumes of his *hortus siccus* (albums of dried plants) are now in the Sloane collection at the Natural History Museum in London.[11]

It was a period in which having a private cabinet of curiosities, which could include art, works of virtu, ethnographic objects and

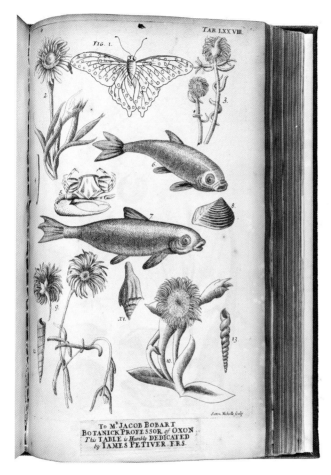

Table LXXVII from Petiver's *Gazophylacium naturae et artis*, engraved by Sutton Nicholls (fl. 1680–1740), including the silverfish and goldfish from China. In hopes of patronage, Petiver dedicated each of his tables to an august figure, in this case Jacob Bobart the Younger, the Botany Professor of Oxford.

exotic flora and fauna, was considered a gentlemanly pursuit and an expression of social status. Petiver, as a humble apothecary, was socially ambitious, and his strategic collecting served him well, leading to a fellowship in the Royal Society and an honorary doctorate from the University of Leiden. Gentlemen exchanging gifts of such objects in the post was also the expression of a norm in the Republic of Letters, a worldwide correspondence network. The Republic of Letters was based on group virtues taken from the ethos of early modern gentlemanly behaviour, characterized by cooperation and modesty, and based on intellectual tolerance, trust, honour and self-control. Fulfilling social obligations, bartering intellectual property, returning favours and sending presents were means of the mutual paying of respect that enhanced a reputation as a gentleman and a scholar. At least that was the way it was supposed to happen. The Republic was not always effective at professionalizing its community of scholars, and cases of insult, plagiarism and even impersonation could occur.[12] To prevent misunderstandings and disappointment, Petiver even published a guide on how to acquire and keep specimens. Although he was one of the first to provide such a guide, keeping specimens in rum, brandy or salt water – as he suggested – significantly discoloured plumage and fur.[13]

Where Petiver got his goldfish is uncertain, but it was probably through such a correspondence network. Next to his *Gazophylacium* entries for the goldfish, he also listed creatures such as a 'brown luzone butterfly with greenish spots that Father Kamel lent me'. Georg Joseph Kamel (1661–1706) was a Jesuit pharmacist stationed in the Philippines at the turn of the eighteenth century, and as historian Sebastian Kroupa has shown, in the late 1690s Kamel had a correspondence network extending from the Spanish colonies in the New World to London which included figures such as Petiver, John Ray and Willem ten Rhijne (1647–1700), a Dutch physician stationed in Batavia.[14] Petiver also knew James Cuninghame (fl. 1698 –1709), an East India Company surgeon in China, so it is possible that the fish made their way to London with a member of this group.[15] Exotic animal specimens were symbols of global trade and empire. According to Kroupa, Petiver recruited people who travelled within these networks. In this regard, his target group were the ship's surgeons and, to a lesser extent, captains. This was an obvious choice, as they were typically the most educated men on the ship, enjoyed highest authority and freedom of movement and were closest to the social status of a credible gentleman, all of which were essential qualities for the completion of Petiver's tasks.[16]

Doctors also had the medical and biological knowledge to keep specimens alive, so perhaps a sea captain or doctor was responsible for getting Petiver his live goldfish.

In fact, later in the eighteenth century, the artist, illustrator and naturalist George Edwards (1694–1773) tells us that Chinese goldfish were more common in London largely due to the efforts of sea captains. In 1733 Edwards became bedel of the Royal College of Physicians, in charge of the college's administration, library and collections. This role permitted Edwards to be introduced to the most significant collectors of this day, including those from overseas, who in turn bought his illustrations and books. As a result, in works such as his *Natural History of Uncommon Birds* (1743–51), he was able to draw and engrave many rare specimens in the ownership of others, making of them in his words, 'a natural and accurate portrayal'.[17] As Arthur MacGregor has noted,

his practice of carefully acknowledging the source of each of his subjects sheds considerable light on the extent to which exotic birds and animals were to be found in the possession of a range of owners from wealthy grandees to humble citizens, as well as specialist traders who emerged to supply this growing market.[18]

Edwards indicated that goldfish 'were generally unknown in England till the Year 1728, when a large Number of them were brought over in the *Houghton* Indiaman, Captain Philip Worth, Commander, and presented by him and Manning Lethieullier, Esq to Sir Matthew Decker'.[19]

Decker (1679–1749), who wrote works on early economics, was a wealthy Dutch merchant, Lord Mayor of London, a baronet, an MP and director of the East India Company. He had a penchant for exotic flora and fauna, his Dutch gardener Henry Telende cultivating the first British-grown pineapple in his garden at Pembroke Villa.[20] Decker enlarged the house and created an exceptional garden. John Macky in his *Journey Through England* (1722–3) wrote,

> The longest, largest, and highest Hedge of Holly I ever saw, is in this garden, with several other Hedges of Ever-greens, Visto's cut through Woods, Grotto's with Fountains, a fine Canal running up from the River. His Duckery, which is an oval Pond brick'd round, and his pretty Summer-House by it to drink a Bottle, his Stove-houses, which are always kept in an equal heat for his Citrons, and other Indian Plants, with Gardeners brought from foreign Countries to manage them, are very curious and entertaining. The house is also very large a-la-modern, and neatly furnished after the Dutch way.[21]

Perhaps the goldfish were in Decker's fountains. He certainly presented the fish to various friends elsewhere in England, where they were kept for ornament in shallow ponds.[22]

The story of the transit of the goldfish to England on the *Houghton* is an interesting one. The *Houghton Indiaman* (named for Houghton Hall, the family home of Sir Robert Walpole), which brought Decker the goldfish, first began service for the East India Company in 1738. It was a 460-tonne ship, with thirty guns and a crew of 92.[23] It was carrying 1,339 piculs of lead (a picul was 113.5 lb (60.5 kg), so 81 tonnes) and a thousand pieces of perpetuano (coarse, durable woollen fabric, sometimes used for coat linings).[24] The *Houghton* departed London on 16 January 1739, arriving at Whampoa (Pazhou Island) on 20 July, making the outbound journey of 25,248 km (15,689 mi.) in record time. In China, the *Houghton* sold its cargo to Teinqua, a Hong merchant using funds to purchase green tea (Hong merchants were Chinese merchants 'authorized by the Chinese government to act as liaison to British traders in Canton').[25] The *Houghton*, after docking at St Helena until its homeward departure in July 1740, also brought back raw and finished silk, cotton cloth, porcelain and a few goldfish.[26]

Edwards confirmed the origins of the fish as St Helena, having previously been taken there from China:

> They vary infinitely in their Colours and Marks, as do all Domestick Animals; they have been propagated and greatly increased in the Island of St Helena; from whence they are now brought by all our India Ships that touch there. They keep them in small Ponds and Basons in China for the Amusement of the Ladies, and other curious Persons. Those propagated with us are generally of a deader Colour than what are brought from China, or St Helena.[27]

Edwards also noted that the fish, some with single tails, some with double, were bred by 'several curious' London gentlemen including Charles Lennox, Duke of Richmond, who had a 'large Chinese earthen Vessel full of these Fish, brought alive to England. I drew some of them for this Grace, who permitted me to make Draughts for myself, with Leave to make them Publick'.[28]

209

Charles Lennox, grandson of King Charles II and Louise de Kérouaille, Duchess of Portsmouth, kept his goldfish at Goodwood House in West Sussex. Goodwood was set in extensive gardens of some 445 hectares (1,100 ac), including 80 hectares (200 ac) of parkland, and it was populated with several buildings, including a pedimented temple to house Roman antiquities, such as the Neptune and Minerva Stone, dug up in Chichester. To the north of the estate, the duke had a shell house, decorated by the Duchess of Richmond and her daughters with West India shells.[29] Lennox was a curious, rather bluff individual, enthusiastic about antiquities, antiquarianism and the new natural philosophy or 'new science', exchanging letters with his good friend Royal Society president Martin Folkes (1690–1754). On 12 November 1732, Lennox wrote to Folkes: 'do dear Folkes [come to Goodwood] if you can; & pray bring a small reflecting Telescope with you, that I would have you buye for me; & some prisms, & any other things to Conjure with'.[30] On another occasion, Lennox wrote to Folkes, 'I want a whirly=gig, who can I apply to better than our President? by a Whirly=gig, I mean a sort of a dial or compass that (with a hand) shews the winds, by being turn'd by a weathercock, a top of the house of Chimney.'[31]

It is probably not surprising that along with collecting strange instruments, Lennox collected strange animals, creating a famous menagerie at Goodwood to house his goldfish and other creatures from all over the world. Lennox included in his list

5 wolves, 2 tygerrs, 1 lyon, 2 lepers [leopards]; 1 sived cat [civet cat], a tyger cat, 3 foxes, a Jack all, 2 Greenland Dogs, 3 vulturs, 2 eagles, 1 kite, 2 owls, 3 bears, 1 large monkey, a Woman tygerr, 3 Racoons, 3 small monkeys, armadilla, 1 pecaverre and 7 caseawarris.[32]

'The Gold-fish from China', in George Edwards, *Natural History of Uncommon Birds and of Some Other Rare and Undescribed Animals* (1743–51).

The menagerie became a tourist attraction to the extent that Henry Foster, Richmond's steward, complained in 1730, 'We are very much troubled with Rude Company to see ye animals. Sunday last we had 4 or 5 hundred good and bad.'[33]

Like the duke, Edwards himself bred goldfish, stating in his *Gleanings of Natural History* (1760): 'The Chinese Fish I have kept alive twenty months in a bason of water: it is drawn from life, of its natural size. It had no fins on the bank, but had little risings on the middle of the back in the place where the fins generally are'.[34] The fish had red fins and a red double tail, and the colour of its 'back was dusky inclining to green, which gradually change into a yellow or golden colour on its underside'. This may have been the eggfish (*dan-yú*), a variety going back about eight hundred years in Chinese goldfish breeding, believed to be an ancestor of the ranchu, celestials and lionheads. It lacks a dorsal fin, and all fins except the caudal fin are small. And, inveterate artist as he was, Edwards did a hand-coloured engraving of his fish, alongside portrayals of a frigate bird (possibly *Fregata magnificens*) and a piece of red seaweed he observed.

After describing the duke's goldfish, Edwards predicted of the species that 'in a few years it is probable, we shall have them in our Rivers'. He was absolutely right. The fish quickly became endemic to England. As the naturalist Thomas Pennant announced in 1776, 'these fish are now quite naturalized in this country, and breed as freely in the open waters as the common carp'.[35] In the 1750s, five ornamental fishponds in Halswell Park were stocked with goldfish, gudgeon and trout. Sir Charles Kemys Tynte (1710–1785) created the pleasure garden, considered one of the finest landscape gardens in Europe.[36]

Even Horace Walpole (1717–1797), the author of the world's first Gothic novel (*The Castle of Otranto*) and youngest son of Sir Robert Walpole (Britain's first prime minister), had goldfish at

This illustration was part of George Edwards's study of the frigate bird, possibly *Fregata magnificens*, with a Chinese goldfish below and a specimen of red seaweed behind.

The Manofwar-bird and the Chinese Fish, &c. all etched on the copper plate from life, by George Edwards, July the first. A. 1758.

309

Strawberry Hill, his remarkable Gothic Revival castle. Though he would eventually abandon his interest in Chinese art and aesthetics for the Gothic, Walpole was an 'early and ardent convert' to the fashion for chinoiserie, a pan-European phenomenon that occupied an exciting and exotic new space between 'reigning discourses of classical taste and polite bourgeois culture'.[37] The fad was especially prevalent because 'far more was known about China in early-eighteenth century Europe than about any other distant port of call', and China came to heavily influence the sociocultural imagination.[38] Chinoiserie was an expression of the exotic and of empire, but it also offered an alternative form of aesthetic expression.

Walpole received a copy of the Jesuit Jean-Baptiste Du Halde's *General History of China* in his first year at Cambridge from Lord Hervey, and he was enthralled, becoming an ardent Sinophile. But his interest in Chinese art was eclectic, as in the 1750s he conflated the Gothic and Chinese styles as giving a 'whimsical air of novelty', as he explained to Horace Mann.[39] Not surprisingly, Walpole gave his prized Chinese goldfish bowl pride of place on a Gothic pedestal in Strawberry Hill's Great Cloister.

From 1740 to 1760, there were advance notices of publication of Edme-Louis Billardon de Sauvigny's *Histoire naturelle des dorades de la Chine* (1780), one of the first books about goldfish in a European language, which reflected the fashion for things Chinese and showed how Walpole was a harbinger of fashion. The French had goldfish from the mid-eighteenth century, imported by the French East India Company and arriving at the port of Lorient.[40] Folklore said that King Louis XV gave some to his mistress Madame de Pompadour, Jeanne-Antoinette Poisson (1721–1764), a golden fish for a golden girl, a pun on her name. This exquisitely illustrated monograph depicts, in full size, 88 hand-coloured engravings of goldfish kept in the imperial aquaria and ponds in Beijing, copied by

Nicholas Martinet, *graveur de cabinet du roy*, and his son Aaron from a Chinese scroll that was sent from Paris to Peking in 1772. The fish look as though they are moving in the water, a revelation for European artists who tended to portray fish as static.

Walpole also delighted in giving live goldfish as gifts, a means of social exchange that could display his knowing good taste. In fact, Walpole's friend, the artist Richard Bentley, had carried a dozen of Walpole's fish to London 'in a decanter' to give as presents, and Walpole told Field Marshal Henry Seymour Conway that the arrival of his goldfish was imminent:

> the fish are apprised they are to ride over to Park-place [Conway's home at Remenham in Berkshire], and are ready booted and spurred; and the moment their pad arrives, they shall set forth. I would accompany them on a pillion if I were not waiting for Lady Mary [Lady Mary Churchill] who as desired to bring a poor sick girl here for a few days to try the air. You know how courteous a knight I am to distressed virgins of five years old, and that my castle-gates are always open to them.[41]

In May 1755 Walpole wrote to Bentley:

> I have lately given Count Perron some goldfish, which he has carried in his post-chaise to Turin: he has already carried some before. The Russian minister has asked me for some too, but I doubt their succeeding there; unless, according to the universality of my system, every thing is to be found out at last, and practised every where.[42]

Walpole's universality thesis turned out to be correct, as goldfish were in Russia at the end of the eighteenth century. On 1 April

1791, Prince Potyomkin, the favourite of Catherine the Great, gave a banquet in her honour in his Winter Garden, where goldfish in bowls were part of the lavish decorations.[43]

From the frequency with which the fish appeared in his correspondence, it can be seen that they were an integral and lively part of Walpole's life at Strawberry Hill, and even contributed to a famous poem. Walpole wrote to George Montagu on 6 June 1752 that: 'We lead quite a rural life, have had a sheep-shearing, a hay-making, a syllabub under the cow, and a fishing of three *gold fish* out of Poyang.' 'Poyang' was what Walpole called his goldfish pond, after a reference in Du Halde to a large lake in Jiangxi province celebrated for its goldfish; the fish were 'Poyangers'. The fish were 'for a present to Madam Clive . . . Mr Bentley is with me, finishing the drawings for Gray's Odes; there are some mandarin-cats fishing for gold fish, which will delight you.'[44]

He was referring to his friend (and possibly lover) Thomas Gray, who wrote a poem on the occasion of Walpole's tabby cat Selima having a fatal accident in Walpole's prized Chinese gold-fish bowl. The 'Ode on the Death of a Favourite Cat, Drowned in a Bowl of Gold Fishes' was illustrated by Richard Bentley, and published to great success. The poem opened: ''Twas on this lofty vase's side/ Where China's gayest art has dy'd/ The azure flow'rs that blow/ Demurest of the tabby kind/ The pensive Selima reclin'd, Gaz'd on the lake below.'

The greedy Selima who gazed at the goldfish, would, like Narcissus admiring his image, come to a bad end. The rest of the poem, in the mock heroic style, its iambic tetrameter of over-blown pomp, was a parody of funeral odes popular in the era, ending with the warning:

From hence, ye beauties, undeceived,
Know, one false step is ne'er retrieved,

And be with caution bold.
Not all that tempts your wandering eyes
And heedless hearts, is lawful prize;
Nor all that glisters, gold.

The eccentric Walpole had the first stanza of Gray's poem 'engraved on the pedestal for the fatal porcelain tub, which remained on view in his Strawberry Hill House'.[45]

And so, the trope of the cat staring into the goldfish bowl in the visual arts was born. Artist and poet William Blake (1757–1827) quickly followed suit, paying his homage to the unfortunate Selima, and portraying the fish as surrealistic evil temptresses. The poet Anna Seward (1742–1809), in her 'An Old Cat's Dying Soliloquy', even wrote some verse from the cat's perspective: 'Thy Selima shall bend her moping head/ Sigh that no more she climbs, with grateful glee/ Thy downy sofa, and thy cradling knee/ Nay e'en at founts of cream shall swear/ Since thou her more lov'd Master, art not there'.[46]

But one of the best employments of the theme of thwarted cat and the temptations of the goldfish bowl was in the work of Nathaniel Hone (1718–1784), a rival of Sir Joshua Reynolds. Hone painted a portrait of the notorious Catherine Maria 'Kitty' Fisher (c. 1741–1767). Daughter of a German silver-chaser who settled in Soho, Kitty became the most celebrated member of the London demi-monde, a courtesan who used painted and printed images to maintain her celebrity and to appeal to her rich clientele. Her suitors included Admiral Augustus Keppel, Admiral Lord Anson and General Ligonier, and she was extravagant in her tastes, having been rumoured to eat a £100 note on a slice of buttered bread. Casanova, the notorious Italian seducer, was offered an opportunity to bed Fisher for ten guineas, but he refused because she did not speak French.[47] Not surprisingly, when this portrait was

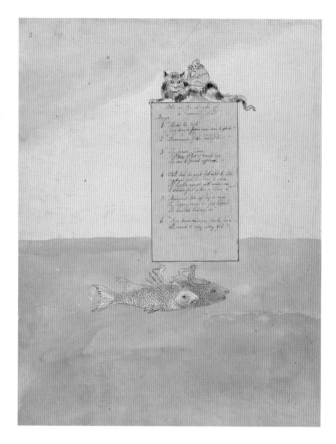

William Blake, 'The Poems of Thomas Gray', Design 7, *Ode on the Death of a Favourite Cat*, c. 1797–8, verso watercolour with pen and black ink and graphite on moderately thick, slightly textured, cream wove paper with inlaid letterpress page.

exhibited, the *Public Advertiser* noted it was 'a portrait of a Lady whose charms are well known to the town ... The artist has ingeniously attempted to indicate her identity: by her side a kitten is attempting to get fish from a goldfish bowl – Kitty Fisher.'[48] Hone's portrait is also one of the first to show the iconic glass goldfish bowl with glinting fish and window reflections, painted to show off his painterly virtuosity and increase his own fame.

The portrait was also, of course, a knowing cultural referent to the Thomas Gray poem, as Kitty herself had a poem dedicated to her entitled 'Kitty's Stream or Noblemen turned Fishermen'. Horace Walpole certainly knew of Kitty, and claimed that she was 'recognized in a London park by both the young Prince Frederick William and his elder brother the Prince of Wales [afterwards George III]'.[49] Kitty is wearing cloth of silver accented with gold,

William Blake, 'The Poems of Thomas Gray', Design 7, *Ode on the Death of a Favourite Cat*, *c.* 1797–8, recto watercolour with pen and black ink and graphite on moderately thick, slightly textured, cream wove paper with inlaid letterpress page.

shimmering like the goldfish. Hone's portrait plays with the enigma of Kitty, whose hair was dark like the hunting feline, as a fisher of men. Or was she being fished herself? Would she, like the cat, drown as a result of her greed, not for a meal, but for riches and narcissistic pleasure? Kitty died aged 26.

Decorative goldfish bowls were becoming prevalent among aristocracy and gentry. In 1781 the famous naturalist Gilbert White noted in a letter to Daines Barrington:

> some people exhibit this sort of fish in a very fanciful way; for they cause a glass bowl to be blown with a large hollow space within, that does not communicate with it. In this cavity they put a bird occasionally; so that you may see a goldfish or a linnet hopping as it were in the midst of the water, and the fishes swimming in a circle round it. The simple exhibition of the fishes is agreeable and pleasant; but in so complicated a way becomes whimsical and unnatural and liable to the objection due to him, 'Qui variare cupit rem prodigialiter unam'.[50]

The Latin phrase is part of a poem from the ancient world, Horace's 'De re poetica'. His verse advised, 'he who wants to vary his subject in a marvellous manner, paints the dolphin in the woods, the boar in the sea. The avoiding of an error leads to a fault, if it lacks skill'.[51] White was obviously not impressed.

Goldfish had also reached the Continent as, from the 1740s onwards, interest in marine zoology grew in Europe. Naturalists like the indefatigable physician Job Baster bred goldfish in the Netherlands. Baster resided in Zierikzee in Zeeland, the least populated area of the Netherlands, consisting of islands and peninsulas, figuratively and literally a backwater. For example, in one of his letters to Linnaeus, Baster wrote, 'Nothing ever

happens here.' To be fair, modern Zierikzee is a charming tourist town, and in Baster's day Zierikzee was significant to the fishing industry, as can be seen on Johannes Blaeu's mid-seventeenth-century map of the town. Zierikzee's connections with the marine world may have sparked Baster's interest in goldfish.

Before his work with goldfish, Baster was best known for his work on marine animals, investigating the venomous organs (called *pedicellariae*) of sea urchins and the anatomy of coral, his work published in the *Philosophical Transactions of the Royal Society*.[52] He was involved in a controversy where he (wrongly) argued that coral served as the habitation of the enclosed creature rather than forming a constituent part of the animal, and he also analysed worms that destroyed the wooden piles of the Dutch seawalls in the 1720s.[53] Baster is the godfather of *Basteria* (reader, pronounce very carefully), the venerable Dutch scientific journal of the Netherland Malacological Society; the journal is devoted to the study of molluscs.

So great was his interest in things marine that, as a hobby, he used shells from his collection to make decorative objects, at that time a fad in various European countries. Within a shrubbery at Goodwood, for example, the Duchess of Richmond and her daughters spent seven years creating a much-admired grotto decorated with shells in patterns 'forming vases and cornucopias of flowers' and with a floor 'paved with marble and horses' teeth'.[54]

Baster's cupboard (in Dutch a *schelpenbuffet*, or scallop buffet), though much more modest in scale, was still sizeable – 318 cm (125 in.) high, 232 cm (91 in.) long and 21 cm (8 in.) deep – and sophisticated in its decorations, encrusted with exotic tropical snail shells reflecting Dutch global trade (*Cypraecassis rufa*, *Chicoreus ramosus*, *Palmadusta asellus*), corals, fossils and ossicles (otoliths) of fish.[55] It is possible that Baster, like Petiver, knew ship captains of the East and West India Companies that brought him shells for payment. Baster's letters to Linnaeus, for example, reveal that he received seeds or new plants from friends living in the Carolinas in North America, and a live herbarium of Javanese plants from Captain Caspar Blaster of the Dutch ship *De Hoop*.[56] At that time there was, however, already a considerable trade in shells and possibly Baster also just bought specimens or acquired them through friends, as he did many other types of *naturalia*. It is striking that, although many cowrie shells have been used in the buffet, there are noticeably few *Monetaria moneta* (money cowries or slave money).[57] For

> centuries before European expansion in the 1500s, cowries were . . . used as a form of currency in some areas – hence the name 'money cowrie'. With the advent of the slave trade to the New World, cowries were among the items that Europeans exchanged with coastal West African groups for slaves. By the early 18th century, hundreds of thousands of pounds of cowrie shells were being exported from South Asia to Europe, often as 'packing peanuts' in the China trade, and then re-exported from Europe to Africa.[58]

By the late seventeenth century, there was a distinct stream of cowrie shells from the Maldives to Balasore and other Indian ports, and then to Europe, primarily London, where private dealers and the East India Company sold the shells to merchants in the African (slave) trade.[59] Money cowries were widely available, but also expensive, which may have limited their use in Baster's *schelpenbuffet*.

The still extant cabinet has ledges for bird sculptures made of shells and a flower vase for Dutch bulbs, also covered in mother-of-pearl from nacreous shells. At the bottom of his buffet is the coat of arms of Baster (jumping greyhound) and his wife Jacoba Vink (climbing lion) in shell mosaic. The shell cabinet was one of the first donations made to the Zeeuwsch Genootschap (The Royal Zeeland Society of Sciences). In 1768 Baster was appointed as a member of the Zeeland Society and in 1773 he wrote to J. W. te Water, the secretary of the Society, that he would like to leave

his 'schelpenbuffet' in the Society on view 'in my big side room
. . . with all the rarities that stand on it'.[60]

In his interests in natural history, Baster followed in the foot-
steps of such illustrious Dutch predecessors as Antonie van
Leeuwenhoek (1632–1723), who was one of the first microscop-
ists. Like Leeuwenhoek, Baster employed an artist, Johannes
Rhodeus, to use hand lenses and microscopy to produce empirical descriptions and drawings of exquisite detail of flora and
fauna in his masterwork, the *Opuscula subseciva* (1759–65). In the
early modern period, this area of Zeeland was a leading centre
of lens crafting and the invention of the telescope and microscope was often credited to Middelburg spectacle-makers like
Hans Lippershey.[61] The longer translated title of Baster's *Opuscula* indicates more clearly what he was using lenses to study; he
adds (modestly): 'A minor work on remaining observations concerning miscellaneous marine animals and plants which spawn
and produce in moderation'. His book had several new discov-
eries (and rather ghastly looking sketches) of fish lice (caligid
copepods), and some rather more attractive illustrations of goldfish and magnifications of their pellucid scales.[62] Baster, like his
English contemporary Henry Baker, experimented with microscope lenses to reduce chromatic aberration (failure to focus), as
well as accessories for the instrument, which allowed for better
magnification of waterborne organisms. In the ceiling of his
house on Havenpark, a plaster cherub is portrayed holding a
mirror and a small telescope, a possible reference to Baster's
interest in optics.

This attention to detail served Baster well in his cultivation of
fish. Although in 1753–4 a number of goldfish (*Goudvisch*) were
introduced to ornamental waters belonging to Count Clifford and
Lord of Rhoon in Holland, they had not managed to breed.[63]
Baster, however, saved the day for the Dutch goldfish when he

inherited a garden, called the Zonnehof (sun garden), with trees and two ponds.

Thanks to the Republic of Letters, Baster cultivated a contact in England and obtained twelve goldfish.[64] Although these all quickly perished in his garden fishponds, probably due to the winter cold, his efforts the following year were much more successful. In the winter of 1759 he introduced sixteen goldfish to his ponds; on 13 June 1760 he saw 'some little fish 4–6 lines long, and of a blackish or swarthy colour. About six weeks later most of them developed silvery or white spots.' He recorded his delight at seeing the fry change to silver and gold, 'with such a spectacular splendour that our best gilt pales by comparison', and observing them under the microscope, 'to see the movement of the Viscera so clearly' and drawing their scales.[65] He even had his prints of the fish for his books flecked in gold to emphasize their beauty, recording the fry's 'grubby green colour' (*graauwagtig groen van couleur*), which was transformed to shimmering silver or white when the fish formed a stripe on its body of 'half a breadth'. Baster also enjoyed watching his goldfish dart and play in the water, and noted that they were not nearly so sensitive to noise or odours as he had been led to believe by reading previous accounts. He recommended the importance of introducing the fish gradually and gently into new ponds rather than just dumping them in, or else the fish would dive to the bottom afraid to come to the surface, and eventually suffocate. Baster learned to lower a bucket of the fish, hanging by a rope, gradually into his ponds, letting the fish swim out of their own accord. This is something breeders do to this day to acclimatize their fish to new surroundings.

Baster noted that some of the best food for the fish was a Dutch waffle soaked in water, boiled egg yolk or lean pork dried in the sun and ground to a powder. Biology and gastronomy indeed were closely related in other ways. He wrote,

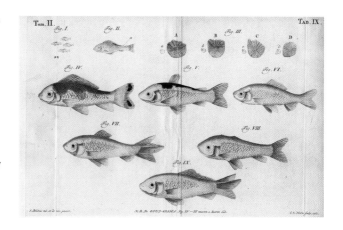

J. Rhodius, 'Studies of freshwater goldfish'. Figure I is a drawing of the fry that are four to five weeks old. Figure II is a more mature fish of 2.5–4 cm (1–1.5 in.) that begins to shimmer silver or white, and forms a stripe on its body of 'half a breadth'. By this point, Baster reported his fry were eating breadcrumbs and water-insects. Figure III, A–D are magnified fish-scales. Figures IV– IX are side views of individual fish, showing a variety of colours and markings at two years of age. The original plate is beautifully picked out in shimmering gold.

I have cooked some of the largest of these [gold]fish, and have eaten them in company with good friends. We tried them with various sauces, but with the so-called 'Eijer Sauce' [egg sauce, probably Hollandaise] they were tastiest, and much better than the common Carp: they were ... fine and much tenderer as some River Fish ... and they do not have any kind of obnoxious bones, like the Voorn [roach], Snoek [pike], etc. They were as delicious baked as Baars [perch].[66]

He was ultimately forgiven for eating his experimental subjects. In 1976 a statue of Baster made by the Zierikzee sculptor Ad Braat was unveiled in the herb garden next to the car park Mosselenboomgaard (the site of the former Zonnehof). It was moved in 2007 to the Havenplein opposite the Baster residence, showing the bemused naturalist holding one of his goldfish, with a few more fish peeping at the surface of one of his ponds.

His breeding experiments, dissections and microscopic observations of the fish were published not only in his *Opuscula*, but in the transactions of the Haarlem Academy using the Japanese name of *king-yo* to describe them. Baster proudly wrote to Carl Linnaeus, whom he hero-worshipped, about his publication, and offered to send fish to Linnaeus if he could find the means to do so quickly and safely.[67] Baster was perfectly sensible to think it could be done, for in the 1720s Daniel Defoe reported that fish were regularly transported alive in England:

For carrying fish alive by land-carriage; this they do by carrying great buts fill'd with water in waggons, as the

Statue of Job Baster, Zierikzee, the Netherlands.

J3.11. 12. 151.

Dried goldfish, *Cyprinus chinensis* (specimen 1853.11.12.151), from the Gronovius Collection. This is a syntype, part of a set of 'type' or 'UR' specimens of equal status, upon which the description and name of a new species is based.

carriers draw other goods: The buts have a little square flap, instead of a bung, about ten, twelve, or fourteen inches square, which, being open'd, gives air to the fish, and every night, when they come to the inn, they draw off the water, and let more fresh and sweet water run into them again. In these carriages they chiefly carry tench and pike, pearch and eels, but especially tench and pike, of which here are some of the largest in England.[68]

Baster never did work out how to send his goldfish to Linnaeus in Sweden, though he did provide a specimen to the Leiden naturalist Laurens Theodorus Gronovius (1730–1777). Gronovius subsequently preserved the goldfish's skin and mounted it on cartridge paper using a method invented by his father Jan Frederik (1686–1762), known for his own *Flora Virginica* featuring dried New World plants. After the fish was gutted, the 'back-bones are then cut assunder, the Fish is to be washed, rubbed till it is dry with a Linen Cloth, and placed upon a Board . . . all the Fins and Tail are to be expanded' with 'minikin pins'. The skin was then sun- or heat-dried, separated from the flesh and pressed flat with parchment paper underneath. The skins were then varnished with a mastic (30 g) copal gum (20 g), sandarac (20 g) and ethyl alcohol (350 cc) mixture, and mounted on folio sheets. Joseph Banks, an eighteenth-century scientist, once owned the collection. The fish skins and their preparation were the subject of a meeting and publication by the Royal Society, and the goldfish skin still survives in the Gronovius Fish Collection at the Natural History Museum in London.[69] The specimen itself is special too, a syntype, a taxonomic name that lets us know it is part of a set of 'type' or 'UR' specimens of equal status, upon which the description and name of a new species is based.

Linnaeus was patient. The Swedish ambassador Nils Palmstierna (1696–1766) arranged for a preserved goldfish (a fantail) to be sent to Linnaeus, who dissected it and described it in the academy's proceedings in 1740.[70] Linnaeus at this point seemed to understand how to take care of the fish, although it was unclear if he had any personal experience, and he had 'received information from someone who knew'.[71] Linnaeus had also spent time in the Netherlands; it may be possible that he learned from Baster.

This information whetted Linnaeus's appetite for live goldfish (although not in the same way as Baster!). To that end, he asked one of his first disciples, the explorer and pastor Christopher Tärnström (1711–1746), to get some specimens, and in 1746 Tärnström went to China on an East India Company trading ship. Linnaeus wrote a letter of instructions from Uppsala, which was characteristically detailed and demanding:

Honorable Sir,

When giving instructions for Mr Tärnström to observe on his East India journey, the following would be useful.

1. To acquire a tea bush in a pot or at least seeds thereof to be kept according to the verbal instructions he has received from me.
2. Seeds from the Chinese mulberry tree with split leaves . . .

13. Live goldfish for Her Royal Majesty.
14. Measurements night and day with a thermometer south of the Equator and in Canton[72]

Sadly, Tärnström drowned off the island of Pulo-Condore, off the coast of what is now Vietnam, and Linnaeus had to console himself again with preserved goldfish, this time from King Adolf Frederick, from the royal ponds of Drottningholm.

However, Linnaeus was luckier with his pupil, the physician and early oncologist Pehr af Bjerkén. Bjerkén was in London, regularly sending the Swede English books of natural history via the good offices of the sea captain Johan J. Fischer. So Linnaeus simply asked Bjerkén to have Fischer send him fish.[73] On 7 October 1750, Bjerkén told Linnaeus that the previous week he had sent the 'goldfishes and the orang-outang' not with Fischer but with Captain Johan Pihlström. He included detailed instructions on how to care for the fish, stressing the importance of changing the water and keeping the tanks clean. It was not made clear what Linnaeus was to do with the orang-utan.

Bjerkén had received the goldfish from Richard Guy. Guy was a wealthy surgeon, the source of his riches being patent medicines for cancer. Bjerkén in fact told Linnaeus 'that he had bought [from Guy] a secret drug against [cancerous] tumours for £3,000', which was a small fortune. Guy advocated non-surgical approaches to oncology using a series of medicines, including the arsenic-containing 'Plunkett's poultice'. The poultice was designed to attack tumours in breast and maxillofacial cancers, stemming from the idea that the poison of the arsenic attacked the poison of the cancer. In 1762 Guy published *Practical Observations on Cancers and Disorders of the Breast*, which claimed over one hundred successful cures with drugs and without surgery. As breast amputation without anaesthesia was absolutely horrific, life-threatening and could offer small hope of a complete cure, many patients came to see him. Guy believed, as did many surgeons and physicians of the eighteenth and nineteenth centuries, that cancer was a modern and stress-related disease that primarily afflicted women.[74] He wrote, 'Women are more subject to cancerous disorders than Men, especially such Women that are of sedentary, melancholic Disposition of Mind, and meet with such Disasters in Life, as occasion much trouble and Grief.'[75]

One of the happier results of Guy's wealth accrued by the desperation of the chronically ill was that he was able to afford goldfish, and a great many, possessing a large pond on his country estate with fifty to sixty swimming about. 'Because of Linnaeus's good reputation', Guy gave Linnaeus the biggest specimens.[76] The following year, Guy kindly sent new goldfish to Linnaeus when some of the first contingent died, and the famous naturalist Daniel Solander (botanist on Captain James Cook's first voyage and librarian for Joseph Banks, president of the Royal Society) arranged the shipment.[77] So, thanks to the generosity of an early oncologist, these goldfish lived, immortalized by Linnaeus in his *Systema naturae* featuring his new system of binomial nomenclature still used to classify every living creature. Linnaeus gave them their scientific name, *Carassius auratus*.

The modern goldfish was born. In the next century, as it was found to be hardy and easy to breed even in colder climes like Sweden, it would transform from something rare and precious into a consumerist commodity where it would swim in the waters of nineteenth-century America. No longer the preserve of the elite or the academic, the goldfish would become a decorative ornament in the home and an icon of childhood.

4 Goldfish by the Million and the Age of Consumerism

The popularity of the goldfish in Victorian England and the United States was inherently bound with consumerist culture of the newly emergent middle class, industrialization and booming foreign trade.[1] The manufacture of round glass fishbowls and the freshwater aquarium, as well as the evolution of scientific aquaculture and commercial goldfish farming, played a role. The opening of the first public aquarium in 1853 in London at the Zoological Gardens at Regent's Park also contributed to the popularity of keeping fish as pets. By the mid-1800s, there was also significant growth in the wholesale trade in pets in the United States, as animal companionship was increasingly democratized.[2] As an example, in the first four decades of the twentieth century before the Second World War interrupted trade, the USA imported 10 million canaries from Germany, where rollers from the Harz mountains were bred for their beautiful voices.[3] Goldfish had a similar boom in popularity.

In England, with the abolition of the glass tax in 1845, pressed-glass goldfish globes became affordable and the glittering fish so popular that during summertime itinerant 'goldfish hawkers' operated in London and in the countryside. They bought their fish from wholesalers in Kingsland Road and Billingsgate, who brought in lots largely from Essex breeders, though some were imported from France, Holland, Belgium and the Indies to 'improve their breed', presumably (although it was not understood at the time) to introduce genetic diversity.[4] Outside the capital the 'goldfish hawkers' received the goldfish by rail, in vessels with air holes. The small fish were sold for two shillings a pair, the globes of 30 cm (12 in.) in diameter costing up to 2s. 6d. In his 1851 book *London Labour and the London Poor*, Henry Mayhew noted that in the summer, 'the gold and silver fish-sellers, who are altogether a distinct class from the bird-sellers of the streets, resort to the country, to vend their glass globes, with the glittering fish swimming ceaselessly round and round'.[5] As the sellers were misinformed that the fish did not need to be fed but could subsist from 'animalcula' in the water, a persistent urban legend noted by naturalist Gilbert White even in the eighteenth century, the fish must have seemed a very attractive pet.[6] In the winter, the sellers took up other trades such as costermongering (fruit and vegetable selling); one goldfish-seller specialized in pineapples.[7] Mayhew estimated, based on his counts of street sellers, that in the mid-nineteenth century 131,040 fish were sold per year to the public, at a cost of £6,552.[8] That's a lot of goldfish.

Mayhew also noted that clientele for the fish were generally private 'ladies and gentlemen', but also shopkeepers 'that often show goldfish and flowers in their shops' for the genteel. George Dunlop Leslie's (1835–1921) painting *The Goldfish Seller* supports Mayhew's observation. He portrayed a peddler offering a goldfish for sale to a family in suburban London, with the potential bourgeois buyers illustrated as sceptical and bemused at this benign interloper. The artist ensured that the peddler, and by extension the working class, had 'been sanitized, ordered and made acceptable to the middle-class audience', who bought his pictures 'from the sunny side of English domestic life'.[9] At a time when respectable women who were thoroughly indoctrinated in the nineteenth-century 'cult of true womanhood' did not feel comfortable going out in public to shop, where country roads were not paved, or there was little in the way of accessible retail options, the goldfish swam to them.

Itinerant goldfish peddlers were in the United States too, and it was the occupation of immigrants. From the 1820s to the 1880s, nearly 250,000 German Jews emigrated to America, and most 'opted for on-the-road peddling as their start-up occupation in their new American home. Those who did not peddle owned shops, peddler warehouses and manufactured the goods that Jewish peddlers sold'.[10] Many of these peddlers had success stories, becoming wealthy merchants; the riches of Solomon R. Guggenheim, Henry Lehman and Gimbels department store resulted from their early efforts as peddlers. Like Mayhew's photojournalism on London street-sellers, in 1905 the New York newspaper the *Saturday Evening Mail* published a Christmas feature on the city's festivities, 'Among the Sidewalk Vendors at Holiday Time'. The article featured 'Italian women selling lace of their own manufacture, canary sellers and men selling goldfish, displaying them on tripod stands'. The image of American immigrants scratching for a living is a world away from Leslie's idealized painting.

We do not really know when the fish made its first appearance in America, although it can be safe to say that P. T. Barnum wrongly claimed the credit when in 1842 he opened the first American public aquarium in Manhattan. (To be fair, he did achieve the miraculous feat of keeping a white whale in water pumped in from the East River.) He promoted the fish as a freak of nature, an ichthyologic counterpart to the bearded lady and polydactyl man exhibited as sideshows. We can, however, narrow down the dates when the goldfish really swam to America by an examination of *Webster's Dictionary*.[11] Noah Webster's first edition of his *Compendious Dictionary of the English Language* of 1806 has

no listing for goldfish, but does intriguingly have listed under the term 'Adonis' 'a charmer, a small gold colored fish'.[12] In 1817 the goldfish definitively appeared in the dictionary, defined as a fish having a 'glossy gold colour', and by 1828 the definition was very specific, indicating it was a well-known creature in America with known origins that was of general and zoological interest: 'of the genus *Cyprinus*, of the size of a pilchard, so named from its bright color. These fishes are bred by the Chinese, in small ponds, in basons or porcelain vessels, and kept for ornament.' By 1869 the definition had altered again:

George Dunlop Leslie (1835–1921), *The Goldfish Seller*, oil on canvas.

Goldfish merchants on Sixth Avenue, image from New York's *Saturday Evening Mail*, 30 December 1905.

It is a small fish of the genus *Cyprinus* (*C. auratus*) so named for its colour, being like that of gold. It is a native of China, and it said to have been introduced into Europe in 1691. It

97

Calico comet goldfish.

is often kept in small ponds or glass globes, as an object of curiosity or ornament.

Though goldfish had been in the United States for some time, in 1878 America 'officially' imported goldfish from Japan, presented by the indefatigable Rear Admiral Daniel Ammen to the United States Commission of Fish and Fisheries. In addition to having a glittering military career, Ammen also wrote several books of the history of warfare, edited the letters of President Ulysses S. Grant, and, more surprisingly, authored *Country Homes and Their Improvement* (1885), where he said of a pond that 'there is probably no one feature attached to a country home that will be found more useful and attractive to the young and old'.[13] Ammen himself maintained a farm near Beltsville, Maryland, and kept goldfish ponds, purportedly refusing '$5,000 cash for the finest specimen in his collection'.[14] As a result of his gift, the breeding of goldfish was carried out in government nurseries, some in the lots near the Washington monument, and government worker Hugo Mullert developed the comet goldfish as a distinctive American breed. Comets have a deeply forked single tail, long flowing fins and tend to be slimmer and smaller than common goldfish, with a more pointed appearance and a larger variety of colouration, the blue patches particularly prized.

Because the Fisheries Commission was a new government division, it decided a little publicity drive was in order and subsequently offered free goldfish to residents of Washington, DC. A written request to one's congressman resulted in a free goldfish

Government goldfish collected at the Carp Ponds, Washington, DC, on 24 January 1878 by William Palmer, drawing by H. L. Todd.

THE GOLD FISH.

Carassius auratus (L.), Bleeker.

Drawing by H. L. Todd, from No. 22107, U. S. National Museum, collected at the Carp Ponds, Washington, D. C., January 24, 1878, by William Palmer.

in a bowl.[15] Unfortunately, the campaign was a little too successful. On 23 November 1894, the broadsheet *Alexandria Gazette and Virginia Advertiser*, in an article entitled 'No More Free Gold-fish', stated:

> Citizens who apply to the Fish Commission in Washington for goldfish will be doomed to disappointment in future. The commission has found it necessary to curtail the generous and gratuitous distribution of these fish which has come, during the past five years, to be a large part of the institution. In the future, goldfish will be furnished only to State commissions, to parks, and for public uses generally … This step has been forced upon the commission by the steady increase of the demand for goldfish, which has grown until it overtaxes the forces of the bureau and interferes with more important work. The custom of giving them away has grown from small beginnings ten years ago, until during the past five seasons the annual output has amounted to about 20,000 fish.[16]

In 1912 Washington, DC, newspapers were still writing reminders that Uncle Sam no longer provided free fish, noting requests were 'so frequent that the commission has a circular letter that the United States does not supply goldfish on application'. The disappointed applicant instead could see 'the Public Goldfish' in the 'fountain basins in the White House grounds, in Franklin Park, in the west fountain of the Capitol, the fountains in the courts of the House and Senate office buildings and in numerous other government buildings and reservations'.[17] Even with the support of Uncle Sam, government goldfish died for an unexpected reason: in 1964 operators of the memorial fountain at President Franklin Delano Roosevelt's 'little White House'

realized that the copper in the 2,189 pennies that had been tossed into the fountains, which were used as wishing wells, was killing the fish.[18]

Well before the U.S. government's involvement, goldfish were common enough in American public ponds outside Washington, DC. At the turn of the twentieth century, the fountain in Union Square in New York sported goldfish, and minor crime commonly occurred when newsboys or newsies fished them out of the pond as it was being drained, here caught in the act by a photographer in December 1908.

By the mid-twentieth century, this sort of tomfoolery became a mainstay of American popular documentary photography. In 1942 Private First Class John C. Byrom Jr, of Waco, Texas, serving in the U.S. Signal Corp, was photographed trying to catch a goldfish

Catching goldfish in Union Square, New York, December 1908.

in the marble-lined pool at the approach to the Taj Mahal. Observing his antics were Corporal Anthony J. Scopelliti and Private First Class Ray Cherry, as well as several amused Indian men. The women did not look so sure. In an attempt to humanize the American armed forces, the exotic and sacred met with mundane sightseeing in the midst of international conflict. And boys never do quite grow up.

By the 1920s, many small towns in the United States had public goldfish ponds and grottos in pleasure gardens. One of the more idiosyncratic was 'Mrs Sunday's Goldfish Grotto' in Winona, Indiana, on Twelfth Street near the home of the famous Christian evangelist Billy Sunday and his wife Nell, known as 'Ma' Sunday. Billy Sunday was a leader of the Chautauqua adult education movement, and his Arts and Crafts-style bungalow was a centre of pilgrimage for his followers and eventually a museum. From the 1900s to the 1970s, thousands attended the concerts, lectures, sermons and educational classes of the Chautauqua in Winona, as well as Brethren Church conferences and Billy Sunday camp meetings, some held at the nearby Grace Theological College and Seminary. Nell 'Ma' Sunday outlived Billy and all their children and, before she died in 1957, she expressed her desire that the home remain untouched as a testament to the Sundays' ministry.[19] Mrs Sunday's Goldfish Grotto was an accompanying attraction for attendees of the Chautauqua who also would visit the Billy Sunday Tabernacle, the bathing beach, Rainbow Point, Bethany Girls' Camp, Winona Hotel, the Lily Pond and Kosciusko Lodge. The Grotto was a large open subterranean room made from native fieldstone in a circular shape, and the water flowed out via a concrete spillway and passed under a small stone bridge with goldfish in the centre pool. The historian W. A. (Bill) Firstenberger, who was the curator of the Billy Sunday Museum, described the origins and significance of the grotto:

Agra vicinity, India, c. 1942. Private First Class John C. Byrom, Jr., of Waco, Texas, trying to catch a goldfish in the marble-lined pool at the approach to the Taj Mahal. Observing are Corporal Anthony J. Scopelliti and Private First Class Ray Cherry.

Four young girls playing by a goldfish pool, Victorian greeting card, c. 1880.

The grotto springs feature was originally built in the 1890s by the landowner adjacent to the Illinois. By the late 1920s, however, the Sunday family was maintaining and using the grotto springs, and at one point Nell even dammed the outlet of the free-flowing spring to create a pond in which she raised goldfish. The outdoor terrain was, for the Sundays, merely an extension of the home's interior. From the informal interior with natural textured burlap walls, through the open-air sleeping porches, onto the terraced landscape, the Sunday property functioned as a continuous spectrum of the natural environment.[20]

The grotto must have given new meaning to that biblical phrase 'the fishers of men' (Matthew 4:19).[21] Mrs Sunday's Goldfish Grotto was eventually filled in with concrete in the 1980s (ye gods and little fishes!) but postcards of it still survive.

In the private sphere, goldfish became living parlour and garden ornaments for the leisured middle class. *Godey's Lady's Book* of 1850 notes:

> Few objects can be more ornamental or amusing than a glass globe containing gold fish . . . the two mediums, glass and water, assisted by the concavo-convex form of the vessel, magnify and distort them; besides, we have the gratification of introducing another element and its beautiful inhabitants into our very parlours and drawing rooms.[22]

The goldfish bowl appears repeatedly in Victorian still-lifes and in paintings of domestic interiors with the housewife, termed the 'angel of the house', looking at the goldfish in a state of reverie. The term 'angel of the house' is from the title of a popular poem of

Benjamin Fawcett, 'Golden and Bronze Carp', in Walter Houghton's *British Fresh-water Fishes*, vol. I (1879). The specimens figured were supplied by Mr Masefield, of Ellerton Hall. It also was the only plate of fish portrayed live; Houghton may have realized humans could develop emotional attachment to goldfish.

1854 by Coventry Patmore (Patmore saw his angel-wife as a model for all women). It is shown as an ornament on the piano, the 'musical fruit of middle-class prosperity', with women performing songs with accompaniment intended for home music-making.[23] A portrayal of two sisters at the piano with its goldfish bowl by Boston artist Mary Brewster Hazelton has a loose impressionistic style that was greatly admired by John Singer Sargent.[24] The composition is unusual and Hazelton cleverly places the globe to capture and refract the soft light source from the window. The passing beauty of the music echoes the passing beauty of illumination. The acquisition of pianos in large numbers vastly extended the market for drawing-room ballads, and standardized 'the genre as a song with piano accompaniment (rather than, say, harp)'.[25] Like the goldfish bowl, the mahogany or rosewood piano was, in the early nineteenth century, a piece of decorative luxury, but with cheaper cottage pianos being produced in the mid-1800s, the instrument eventually became commonplace in the middle-class home.

Some of these drawing-room ballads even involved goldfish in their bowls. 'The Amorous Goldfish' was a song in the 1896 Victorian musical comedy *The Geisha, a Story of a Tea House,* which opened at Daly's Theatre in London's West End, and it had the second longest run of any musical at that time, even coming to America. The musical then spread itself

> even further abroad, and with more success, than any other previous English-language piece, not excepting the works of Gilbert and Sullivan, had done, becoming one of the most popular shows in Central Europe (Keller's statistical survey of 1921 rates it behind only Die Fledermaus, Die lustige Witwe and Das Dreimäderlhaus) and remaining in the repertoire there until quite recently.[26]

James Cadenhead (1858–1927), *Lady with a Japanese Screen and Goldfish (The Artist's Mother)*, 1886, oil on canvas.

After the musical's stage debut, Polyphon Musikwerke in Leipzig, Germany, founded by Brachhausen & Rießner, put 'The Amorous Goldfish' on its mechanical disc-playing music boxes, which were exported worldwide. Brachhausen later left Polyphon, founding the Regina Music Box Company in New Jersey and laying the foundation for the significant boom in the music industry and later the gramophone industry in the United States.

The producer of *The Geisha*, George Edwardes, sought to ride on the coat-tails of the popularity of Gilbert and Sullivan's *Mikado* and appeal to the public's fascination with the Orient and chinoiserie productions on the London stage. The tune 'The Amorous Goldfish', about the unrequited love between a Japanese goldfish in her bowl and the military officer who kept her, was the biggest hit of the show. The main character in the musical was Lieutenant Reggie Fairfax of the Royal Navy, lonely without his fiancée Molly. He strays by going to the 'Tea House of Ten Thousand Joys' and meets, befriends and kisses the beautiful geisha O Mimosa San. O Mimosa, however, is in love with Katana, a soldier, so she discourages his advances with her tale of the 'Amorous Goldfish'. The 'Amorous Goldfish' was doomed to fall in love with her keeper, but she was gradually forgotten and subsequently starved when he, in turn, fell in love with a fellow human. Some careless soul even knocked over her bowl accidentally, and 'the poor little

LE POISSON ROUGE

C'était dans un ballon de verdâtre cristal.
Une bête aux couleurs d'or, d'argent et de brique,
Plus immobile encor que celles qu'on fabrique
Pour pendre au bout d'un jonc, sur les quais, en métal.

Mon doigt l'ayant tiré de son repos royal,
Cet être fit le tour de sa sphère hydropique,
Mais sans ardeur, et tel, en un cirque olympique,
Un coursier trotte sous l'œil de Mossieu Loyal.

Puis, soudain, étirant ses minuscules nageoires,
Cet animal cyprin bâilla comme un lecteur
De... Je passe les noms du livre et de l'auteur.

Votre trépin semblait lui conter des histoires,
Et ce penser troublant votre humble serviteur,
J'ouvris à deux battants, à mon tour, les mâchoires.

The ubiquitous goldfish bowl in the family home, here in a French children's book of 1885, E. D'Hervilly and Gustave Fraipont's *Les Bêtes a Paris*, dedicated to different types of animals.

"Geisha."
Wallner-Theater.

Carl Beckersachs

Mia Werber

phot. Zander & Labisch.

4536.
Photochemie, Berlin.

fish' ended up dead, cold, still 'in her frock of gold'. O Mimosa implied her refusal of Reggie was an act of self preservation.

Because the goldfish bowl was such a ubiquitous item, it was a common trope in scientific demonstrations in British and American culture by the nineteenth century. Michael Faraday's famous 1848 London lecture 'The Chemical History of a Candle', in which he used a goldfish in a bowl as a prop to demonstrate the role of oxygen in respiration, was publicized in the United States. Goldfish bowls were also used to demonstrate principles of physics in

Zander & Labisch, Karl Beckersachs and Mia Werber in *Geisha*, Berlin, 1910.

'The Amorous Goldfish', sheet music by Sidney Jones and Harry Greenbank, 1896.

EXPERIMENT WITH FLUIDS.

American science textbooks and popular periodicals.[27] As Katrina Gulliver notes, a 'natural philosophy textbook for schools published in New York in 1838 also mentions them, as part of a physics problem – the refraction of light makes a goldfish in a glass globe appear to be two fishes'.[28] T. O'Conor Sloane, in an 1886 article for *Scientific American*, suspended a goldfish bowl filled with water on a 1.8-m (5.9-ft) twisted cord to demonstrate principles of centrifugal force as an alternative to a more expensive twirling table.[29] Another scientific principle that no one wanted to demonstrate was that sun shining through a goldfish bowl makes a lens powerful enough to set fire to curtains. In 1919 American newspapers announced that houses where goldfish were kept in round bowls would have to pay increased rates for fire insurance.[30]

We also see a more 'scientific' type of housing for goldfish arise in the nineteenth century, namely the aquarium, made possible by cheap plate glass manufacture and new adhesives. The aquarium was proclaimed by the *New York Tribune* as 'new comfortable glass boxes with all the modern appliances . . . modern glass receptacles'.[31] The earliest sealed glass cases created were not for fish, but for plants, invented by the London physician and amateur naturalist Nathaniel Bagshaw Ward (1791–1868). He lived in a rather insalubrious part of London – Wellclose Square in Stepney – and his attempts at growing a fernery in his garden were summarily unsuccessful due to air pollution, the famous London 'pea-souper' fogs. Ward saw that after raising a hawk moth chrysalis in a sealed jar, grass seedlings and a fern sprouted in the soil at its base. His curiosity about how long the plants could survive in a sealed environment led to the development of the Wardian case, the first terrarium. Evaporation from the water condensed on the sides of the jar in the evening, creating a sealed microenvironment and allowing the plants to thrive.

He published a pamphlet about his method, 'The Growth of Plants without Open Exposure to the Air', and an 1842 book *On the Growth of Plants in Closely Glazed Cases*. Plants could now be transported around the world, revolutionizing botany and bioprospecting, and Wardian cases allowed for the British transport of tea plants to Assam and Sikkim, helping to break the Chinese monopoly on the tea trade. A Victorian passion for growing ferns in elaborately decorated Wardian cases in the parlour soon developed.

George Johnston (1798–1855) made similar cases to house sponges and corals 'kept in small vessels . . . the result was so successful that he suggested the possibility of marine aquaria on a more extended scale'.[32] Anna Thynne (1806–1866) was also one of the first to introduce marine aquaria to London in 1846, housing them in a drawing room of Ashburnham House, near Westminster Abbey:

> Having procured some living madrepores [stony corals] when at Torquay, in the autumn of 1846, she placed them in some seawater in a bottle covered with a bladder, and brought them safely to town. They were then transferred to two glass bowls, the seawater being kept aerated by being daily poured backwards and forwards, and being, moreover, periodically renewed by a fresh supply from the coast.[33]

Thynne certainly knew about the importance of oxygenating the water and maintaining homeostatic balance in an artificial environment, as she said in her own account: 'From this time I regularly placed sea-weed in my glass bowls; but, as I was afraid I might not keep the exact balance required, *I still had the water refreshed by aeration*.'[34] Her corals were kept alive with boiled shrimp, and she witnessed the release of ova and sperm from her madrepores: 'The *Caryophylliae* regularly threw out their ova at the usual season. During the day, seven of my adult Madrepores have at intervals been ejecting a whitish-blue fluid, resembling wood-smoke.'[35] Thynne's participation in early aquarium keeping showed that the pastime was not confined to men, and several female authors popularized seaside or aquarium studies, like Ann Pratt in her *Chapters on the Common Things of the Seaside* (1850).[36] But as Silvia Granata notes, 'apart from occasional references, most authors of aquarium manuals clearly have a male readership in mind, especially when they discuss collecting on the beach, which implied getting wet, dirty, or even risking a fall, making it an unladylike activity by Victorian standards'.[37]

On 4 March 1850 Robert Warington (1807–1867) communicated to the Chemical Society his keeping of two small goldfish in fresh water in a 'large glass receiver of about twelve gallons capacity, having a cover of thin muslin stretched over a stout copper wire, bent into a circle, placed over its mouth, so as to exclude . . . the sooty dust of the London atmosphere'. *Vallisneria spiralis*, one of the best oxygen producers among aquatic plants, was planted in the sand and mud at the bottom, 'its roots covered by one of the loose stones' to keep it in place. Five or six pond snails (*Limnaea stagnalis*) were subsequently introduced to eat away green algae.[38] Everything flourished, the *Vallisneria* luxuriant and the fish 'lively, bright in colour' and healthy, and the snails laying eggs that were devoured by the goldfish. The idea of the 'balanced' freshwater aquarium for the keeping of goldfish was born, revealing in his words 'the adjustment of the relations between the Animal and Vegetable Kingdoms, by which the vital functions of both are permanently maintained'.[39] Warington was not a naturalist like his predecessors, but a chemist and, along with other prominent chemists such as Lyon Playfair or Oxford don C.G.B. Daubeny, he was a proponent of chemico-theology.[40] Chemical cycles were thought to demonstrate God's wisdom in creating a self-sustaining world. It was a version of natural theology that saw evidence for the Creator's existence in natural law and the complex intricacies of nature.

Two years later, Warington and Philip Henry Gosse (1810–1888) experimented with marine aquaria, obtaining seawater from the English Channel via an oyster boat that sold shellfish at the Billingsgate fish market.[41] In 1854 Warington and Gosse

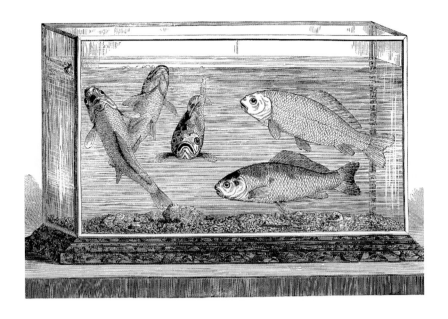

Large goldfish in a household aquarium, from *Cassell's Household Guide*, vol. III (c. 1869). The aquarium has become a staple household item, and the artist has even included the ubiquitous housefly in the tank as prey for the pet fish.

showed how artificial seawater could be made based on Edward G. Schweitzer's analysis of a thousand grains of seawater taken off Brighton. (The weight of a grain, 64,79891 milligrams, was based on that of an idealized seed of cereal.) Gosse simplified the recipe to

Common table salt: 3.5 oz Avoirdupois
Epsom salts: $1/4$oz Avoirdupois
Chloride of magnesium: 200 grains Troy
Chloride of potassium: 40 grains Troy
4 quarts water

Credit for the coining of the term 'aquarium' and its popularization must also go to Gosse and his book *The Aquarium: An*

Unveiling of the Wonders of the Deep Sea (1854). Gosse rejected the term 'vivarium' because it was too general, and 'aqua vivarium' as the name was of 'awkward length and uncouthness, which render it unsuitable for a popular exhibition or domestic amenity'.[42] He worked as a collector providing marine organisms for the Zoological Gardens in Regent's Park, and used his expertise from his book, which advised on the mix of appropriate species for a home tank and detailed collecting practices for plants, fish and molluscs in different English localities.[43] The work was charming, beautifully illustrated with colour plates, lyrically written and interspersed with poetry. Gosse said of prawns, for example, 'their bodies are so pellucid that a lady who was this moment looking at the Tank compared them to ghosts, and their smooth gliding movements aid the similitude'.[44] It was a bestseller and the impetus for the home aquarium craze in England and the United States. According to Henry Nicholls,

In subsequent decades ever greater disposable incomes, a better understanding of the organisms themselves and some very cunning inventions made it easier to overcome the challenges the seawater aquarium posed. The new and widespread interest in the submarine was also met by a proliferation of aquarist societies, specialist publications and stunning public aquaria.[45]

In the second half of the nineteenth century, public aquaria were subsequently constructed in Belfast, Boston, Galway, Edinburgh, Hamburg, Cologne and later at Brighton and at the Crystal Palace Exhibition in 1851.

Some publications advised on how to make aquaria out of found items, for instance *Scientific American*'s 1875 article showing readers how to create a combined 'tasteful little parlour

The ideal home
aquarium,
c. 19th-century
engraving.

aquarium' and Wardian case out of two bell jars and a stand. It was recommended that 'one or two goldfish' should be included to add 'brightness and life to such an arrangement and give life to the water', along with a vase of cut flowers, which would last 'fresh and beautiful for a much longer time than when they are fully exposed to the heated atmosphere of the sitting room'.[46] Another publication suggested 'a darkened bell-glass may be used as part of a more elaborate attempt, in which it may occupy the centre and be surrounded with the ordinary flowering plants with which we are in the habit of decorating our rooms.'[47]

Gosse, however, tended to create aquaria that were similar to the modern models with which we are familiar, made of plate glass, with a bottom slab of slate, and birchwood corners and a frame. 'The glass is set in grooves in the slate and wood, and fastened with white-lead putty . . . a very neat and pretty object for a parlour table, and [it] will hold at least fifty animals appreciable to the senses, provided they be well selected.'[48] Tanks were also being commercially made, Gosse recommending those made by Sanders and Woolcott on Guilford Street in London, who make 'Aquaria from eight feet in length to sixteen inches', including engravings to 'represent some of their forms'. He also noted that Lloyd and Summerfield in Birmingham had some expensive rectangular tanks 'wholly of glass, the bottom, the corner-pillars, and the bars which connect them above, being all of that material', which were in the Crystal Palace Exhibition, and W. A. Lloyd on Portland Road in London was a 'dealer in living marine animals, sea-weeds, natural and Artificial Sea-water and Marine and Freshwater Aquaria' with a price list – tanks were from £1 to an eye-watering £21.[49]

Was the humble goldfish bowl to be supplanted? No, goldfish globes as decorative elements still remained in high fashion in the early twentieth century, but tastes in how to house the fish changed from Victorian exuberance to the pared-down lines influenced by the Art Deco movement, with its tenets of elegance, linearity and simplicity. Goldfish motifs appeared in Art Deco wall hangings and repeating designs, their grace and sinuosity forming pleasing and eye-catching patterns.

There could, however, be too much of a good thing. Grace Wood and Emily Burbank cautioned in their book, *The Art of Interior Decoration* (1919), that

> Bird-cages, dog-baskets and fish globes may become harmonious instead of jarring colour notes, if one will give

'Combined Portable Aquarium and Wardian Case', *Scientific American* (14 August 1886).

a little thought to the matter . . . The fish globe can be of white or any colour glass you prefer, and your fish vivid or pale in tone; whichever it is, be sure that they furnish a needed – not a superfluous – tone of colour in a room or on a porch.[50]

Lovis Corinth, *Dame am Goldfischbassin* (Lady Next to Goldfish Tank), 1911, oil painting.

In its 'Woman's Varied Interests' section of 19 March 1915, the *New York Tribune* placed the article 'Goldfish Bowls as Displayed in the Shops' next to a piece about the new spring dress collections, both consumer goods of fashion. The article explained that while 'One may find ancient Chinese bowls . . . of an inimitable blue ware . . . Very pretty and wholly unusual are the modern glass bowls fashioned after the Poiret precepts'.[51]

Paul Poiret (1879–1944) was a designer with the House of Worth who 'ushered in modernist fashion' with his simple and elegant clothing construction, aligning fashion and modern art.[52] His innovative marketing and advertising, with stencilled *pochoir*

OCTAGONAL TANK.

RECTANGULAR TANK.

Sanders and Woolcott aquaria, in Philip Henry Gosse's *The Aquarium: An Unveiling of the Wonders of the Deep Sea* (1856 edn).

fashion plates and associated lines of cosmetics and perfumes, 'paved the way for contemporary fashion empires and international branding'.[53] His influence and desire to infuse everyday life with elegance and art meant that even goldfish bowls could be designed with taste.

The article went on:

Simply and beautifully painted globes, long-stemmed glasses greatly enlarged, and others Grecian in purity of line, make the most of the beauty of shining glass and colorful contents . . . A very large globe, almost perfectly spherical, has just been completed at a certain shop. This globe is beautifully hand painted in large suggestive lines in black whorl design, with touches of white here and there to enhance the effect of the line. The price of this is $15.[54]

Similarly, a 1908 Italian fashion and glamour postcard by Sergio Bompard shows an elegant maiden feeding her fish and a simple bowl and stand. Poiret would have approved.

If you could not afford goldfish in a Poiret-inspired bowl, you could still be in fashion by owning mechanical Japanese goldfish. This example was distributed in the 1930s by the National Clock Company in New York, whose superintendent was James H. Gerry, who invented and patented the stem-wind attachment for pocket watches.[55] As Japanese fan-tailed fish were introduced to the United States in the 1880s and bred for specialist dealers and connoisseurs, they would have been familiar to consumers. This wind-up clock is described as having

deco numbers on a revolving ball that indicates hours and minutes. While one moving fish ticks out the seconds, the second fish oscillates in a fixed position acting as a

Koloman Moser (1868–1918), *Goldfische Wandbehang* (Goldfish Wall Hanging), print, colour lithograph on paper. An ornament from one of the pioneering Art Deco designers, a sleek and elegant goldfish motif.

pendulum. This gives the appearance that the fish are 'swimming' inside of the fishbowl. This rare clock has six chrome feet similar to a Dominique design that attach to a black painted beveled base with chrome accents and a geometric frieze.[56]

Poiret would not have approved.

We also see a divergence in the late nineteenth and early twentieth centuries between audiences interested in a 'scientific hobby' of exotic aquaria with tropical fish or Japanese goldfish, in America, 'for adult men with deep pockets until the 1920s', and the

124

The stylish lady
and her goldfish
bowl. Illustration
by Georges Barbier
(1882–1932), 'Robe
d'intérieur en soie
brochée, ouverte
sur un dessous de
linon', in *Costumes
Parisiens*, from
*Journal des dames
et des modes*,
no. 61 (1913),
engraving.

general pet owner keeping his or her common goldfish in a bowl as a parlour decoration.[57] There came to be a bit of snobbery from the former about the latter, demonstrated by William T. Innes (1874–1969), who opened his *Complete Aquarium Book* (1917) with the lines:

> A lady wrote the author, I have just bought eight pretty goldfish in a cute little globe. I feed them three good meals a day and change the water often, but they are always at the top of the water with their mouths partly in the air. This makes a little sound. Do you think they are trying to speak to me?

He then remarked about the oxygen-deprived fish,

> the lady should be awarded a medal for crowding the greatest amount of aquarium ignorance into the fewest possible words. Dear Madam: Undoubtedly your fishes are trying to speak to you. Anyone with a slight knowledge would be able to tell what they are saying. It is '*Mistress, have mercy on us; we are suffocating.*'[58]

Innes noted, 'much argument has raged about fish globes, some extremist declaring them a cruelty . . . owing to their shape, the air surface is small . . . the small globe is indeed an abomination'.[59] He then provided measurements of the air-contact surface of different fishbowls, noting, 'In practice the old style globes are almost always overcrowded, and the thing to do is to take goldfish from these and place them in better-formed aquaria.'[60] Despite the proliferation of 'how-to' guides for the beginner, by the 1860s the craze for marine aquaria had subsided in England due to the difficulty of maintenance; saltwater aquaria became the pastime of devoted enthusiasts, and other hobbyists contented themselves with freshwater tanks, often containing goldfish.[61]

Breeding exotic goldfish also became the preserve of connoisseurs, and specialist breeders arose as Japanese goldfish were imported into America in the 1880s. By the 1920s there were a number of newspaper articles devoted to 'Raising Fancy Goldfish', even as a type of 'backyard farm' that yielded great profits. The *New York Sun* reported in 1911 that

> a young man in West Philadelphia has managed to raise enough fancy goldfish in a backyard to pay for a complete professional course in the University of Pennsylvania . . . he at first became interested with a few common goldfish such as are sold at the pet shops for 10 cents each. He found he could raise them in a rain barrel and he decided he could do as well with the fancy varieties. He was fortunate in procuring some fish from a ribbon winning strain and by careful selection of breeders he raised a fine crop of young fish the first season. Some of the best sold at from $20 to $30 each. In less than ten square feet he brought over 500 good fish to marketable size.[62]

The author of the newspaper article interviewed a Philadelphia pet-shop owner on why this young man was so successful, and he replied, 'If you call the goldfish aquarium a fad you must admit it is the biggest fad, the longest lived fad and the most widespread fad by which this faddish country of ours has ever been affected.'[63] American cigarette cards and British tea cards even portrayed goldfish and advised on their care, one advising to 'feed your fish on vermicelli'.[64]

The goldfish 'fad' led to the rise of goldfish competitions among organizations such as the Aquarium Society of Philadelphia who

Japanese goldfish clock. Kitsch that was so wrong and so right. An example of Japanese Art Deco design of the early 1930s, manufactured by the National Clock Company.

'instituted a series of conferences of leading fanciers in order to establish a satisfactory and uniform scale of standards'.[65] Goldfish were judged on points for their type, colour and if they were scaled or nacreous; at the turn of the century, veiltails were particularly prized. Innes in his book *Goldfish Varieties and Tropical Aquarium Fishes* (1917) included official charts with valuation points. As one

Sergio Bompard postcard, c. 1908.

GOLDFISH.

Lidner, Eddy & Claus, *Goldfish*, 1889, lithograph.

would expect, in the case of telescopes and celestials, eye condition and symmetry was important, with other varieties emphasizing brightness or symmetry of colour (blue or lavender in calicos or the shubunkin was desirable) and of course, that ineffable 'style' apparent to a goldfish connoisseur. In November 1914, Joseph E. Bausman won the first annual prize for the best fish bred from the Aquarium Society of Philadelphia, engraved with a veiltail on its front. It was the first medal offered by the society.

Goldfish were so popular that they even became patriotic symbols. The famous Liberty Bond goldfish was exhibited during the First World War. A calico 'gold'-fish with colours of red, white and blue, it was used to draw in the crowds for the Liberty Loan drives of 1917 and 1918.[66] In 1917 President Woodrow Wilson asked directors of American film companies, including Samuel Goldfish of Goldwyn Studios, to help boost support for the war effort by selling government bonds.[67] The directors quickly assented, no doubt partially because many were immigrants of German origin and felt vulnerable, and so they wanted to show they were 'real Americans'.[68] Stars like Mary Pickford, Douglas Fairbanks and Charlie Chaplin toured the United States on a Liberty Loan campaign to get behind Uncle Sam and wheedle money out of their fellow citizens. Although Goldfish changed his name to Goldwyn to soften its Jewish origins, one wonders if he was the brainchild behind the Liberty Bond goldfish. Whatever her

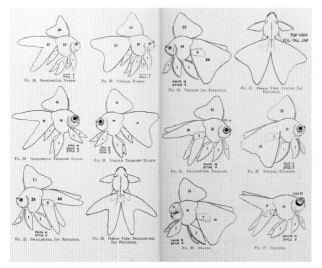

Charts showing ideal figures of the principal goldfish varieties, together with valuation points, by Franklin Barrett, from William T. Innes, *Goldfish Varieties and Tropical Aquarium Fishes* (*c.* 1917).

piscine origins, 'Miss Liberty' grew to be 38 cm (15 in.) long, and she or her descendant was exhibited at the Philadelphia Sesquicentennial celebrations of the 150th anniversary of the signing of the Declaration of Independence.[69] 'Miss Liberty' was valued at $10,000.

Most goldfish, though, became ten a penny, due to the proliferation of huge commercial breeding farms, aquaculture at its most muscular. In 1924 *National Geographic* noted,

> Goldfish farming in Frederick County, Maryland, began about 1889, and in recent years from 35 to 40 establishments have been in operation, employing several hundred . . . the annual output, consisting almost entirely of the common variety, now amounts to between three and four million young fish.[70]

Medal of the Aquarium Society of Philadelphia, November 1914.

There were several establishments in Indiana, and enterprising farmers also bred them as a sideline, like our young man in

Jack Delano, 'Sign at Reitz's Farm advertising goldfish for sale', September 1940, black-and-white photographic negative.

PACKING·THE·FISH·FOR·THE·MARKET.

LARGEST·GOLD·FISH·PONDS~IN·THE·WORLD.

NEAR·ST·PAUL~IND. SHELBY·CO.IND.

Philadelphia, but on a larger scale, as goldfish were hearty enough to survive Midwest and northeastern winters in ponds outside.

Several goldfish farms competed for the claim to be the largest at something, whether the most fish, the biggest ponds or the biggest acreage. Many of them were in Indiana. In 1902 Eugene Shireman transformed his Martinsville swampland into the Grassyfork Fisheries, which became the largest goldfish supplier in the world, producing 2 million goldfish a year, the fry raised on the food of their ancestral home: two tons of Chinese powdered egg yolk per year.[71] Two of the ponds, which covered nearly an acre, were devoted to raising billions of water fleas (*daphnia*) to supplement their diet; the grown fish received ground hominy and cornmeal mush, a far cry from Job Baster's Dutch waffles. A fox terrier named Peggy tackled the water snakes that fed on

'Packing the Fish for the Market, Largest Gold Fish Ponds in the World', near St Paul, Shelby County, Indiana c. 1920.

'The Largest Gold Fish Hatchery in the World. Storage House and a Few of the 200 Ponds, Grassyfork Fisheries', 1925, postcard from Martinsville, Morgan County, Indiana.

the fish. Grassyforks was also a tourist attraction with fountains, a water garden and exotic aquarium fish.

But there were earlier and just as significant contenders for goldfish profligacy. In 1880 William Shoup and Charles Heck founded Spring Lake Fishery, a mile north of Waldron, Indiana, which also claimed to be the largest.[72] By 1914 Spring Lake grew into a site with a hundred ponds on 8 hectares (20 ac). Shoup and Heck supplied pet shops nationwide, breeding common goldfish, as well as telescopes, comets and Japanese fantails, bullfrogs and raising water lilies. At the turn of the century, Spring Lake grossed u.s.$30,000 per annum, and shipped goldfish in cans by horse and cart, rail and steam to the Paris Exposition and the World's Fair in Chicago. Overhead compartments in the transport contained blocks of ice to keep the fish at the proper temperature in the summer heat in order to ensure they survived the journey. When interviewed, Shoup remarked, 'This is [a] more profitable business than raising wheat!'[73] Though lucrative work, it was not glamorous. Shoup's employees were armed with shotguns and patrolled the rounds 'as soon as the bird life is stirring in the morning . . . during the night raccoons, muskrats, and wharf rats put in their work, and their invasion has to be met by putting common rat-traps all around the ponds'. The farm changed owners several times before closing in 1950.

In 1929 there were 21.5 million goldfish bred in the United States, and the wholesale price for one hundred fish of 5 cm (2 in.) in length was $2.50.[74] Goldfish became ordinary, disposable, sold as bait at one dollar for a hundred. By 1968 they were one of twenty species sold as bait, along with topminnows, chubsuckers, tilapia and stone rollers, among others, and in 1978 there were 22,500 hectares in the U.S. devoted to baitfish production, much of it in Arkansas. Anywhere from 250 to 750 broodfish were stocked per hectare. In particular, 'culls' from fancy varieties of fish produced are still used for bait today, as well as for food for

'Looking Over the Gold Fish Ponds', near St Paul, Shelby County, Indiana, c. 1920.

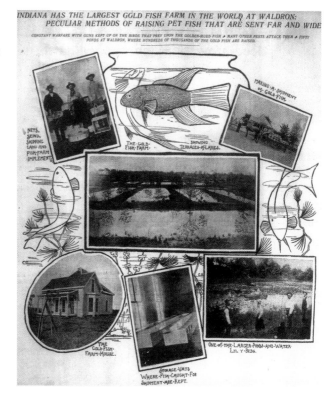

predatory fish in the aquarium trade and for pet snakes.[75] They are no long transported by train, but packed one thousand to a bag of water, filled with oxygen and packed in boxes on dry ice, which will allow them to survive up to a thirty-hour flight as flying fish.

Goldfish were often loss leaders or given away as promotional items in twentieth-century America.[76] Grassyfork Fisheries originated when its founder, Eugene Shireman, was selling washing powder and hit upon the idea of offering a pair of goldfish in a bowl as a premium, a strategy clearly popular with other retailers.[77]

As a result, goldfish ownership among children eventually became universal, a first pet that was easy and inexpensive to maintain, and educational to boot. Goldfish had first appeared in children's picture books in Europe in the eighteenth century, for example in Friedrich Justin Bertuch's *Bilderbuch für Kinder* (Picture Book for Children) published in Weimar, Germany, between 1790 and 1810. Bertuch noted in his preface, 'A picture book is as important and indispensable as a cradle, a doll, or a hobby-horse for a nursery . . . nothing is more important than to accustom the child's eye, from the very beginning, to the true representation of objects.'[78]

But actually owning a goldfish was even better training for empirical observation in children. As *Harper's Young People Weekly* proclaimed in December 1879, by 'caring for them and carefully watching their habits, boys and girls may learn their first lesson in natural history'.[79] Keeping a goldfish may also have offered a first lesson in mortality. My attempts as a toddler to 'soften' my fish Speedy by putting hand lotion in the bowl certainly taught me about death, and that oil and water do not mix. But that probably was not as bad as what happened in 1956 in Laguna Beach, California. The *Memphis World* reported:

Arising at 4.30 to deliver papers, Jim Lansford, lighted the gas heater to warm the house for his wife and daughters. In the dark he didn't notice the goldfish bowl had been placed atop the heater to ward off the night chill. When he returned two hours later, the water was boiling merrily and the goldfish were completely done.[80]

In 1910 when they were more exotic commodities, a pet fish would be posed with an affluent and impeccably coiffed mother and child in a promotional photograph. By 1939 even the barefoot

Advertisement for Kramer's Departmental Flower Stores, in the *Evening Star*, Washington, DC (8 January 1922). The advert was wittily placed next to an article about Canadian Fish treaties.

BARGAIN WEEK AT KRAMER'S
GOLDFISH

3 Live Goldfish in ½-Gal. Bowl. Special this week **45c**

OTHER GOLDFISH OUTFITS

More Fish—Larger Bowl Up to $15

SINGING CANARY BIRDS MODERATELY PRICED

Imported (Rollers) Hartz Mountain and St.-Andreasberg Birds, the world's best singing birds. Come in and hear them.

BLOOMING HYACINTH PLANTS IN PAN $1

5 to 8 Beautiful Blooms, just what you want for home beautifying in the winter months.................

BULBS FOR INDOOR AND OUTDOOR PLANTING

Narcissus Bulbs, 60c Doz. Jumbo Size, $1 Doz.
For indoor planting in sand and gravel.
Lillian Rubrum, Album, Anratum and Magnifican, Golden Banded and Spotted Varieties, each 25c
Lily of the Valley Pips, dozen.........................$1.00
Hyacinths and Tulips, dozen............................ 25c
The above for outdoor planting.
Amaryllis, red and white striped; each....................23c
For indoor planting.

5,000 Flower Baskets,Tumbler cut, special at.. **29c** 3 for only $1.00	**AIR PLANTS** 6,000 Bunches **15c; 2 for 25c**	Imported Hand-Painted Vases .. **29c** $1.00 Value

$5.00 Palms $3.00
$3.50 Palms $1.75
$10.00 Ferns............$5.00
$3.00. Pandanus $2.00
$6.00. Norfolk Island Pines $3.00
$1.00 Fern Dishes 60c
$2.00 Asparagus Plants...$1.00
Artificial Baskets and Centerpieces.. ⅓ **Off**

Kramer's Palm Garden
—in the rear of our Flower Store. Hot Chocolate and Sundaes.

Light Lunches Served
We do not serve extracts in our sodas—we use only Pure Fruits, and charge no more.

KRAMER'S
DEPARTMENTAL FLOWER STORES
916 F Street N.W.   **722 9th St. N.W.**
Open Every Night in the Year Until 12 P.M.

'The Golden Tench, Orfe, Goldfish, and Crooked Fish', in Friedrich Justin Bertuch, *Bilderbuch für Kinder*, vol. I, 2nd edn (1801).

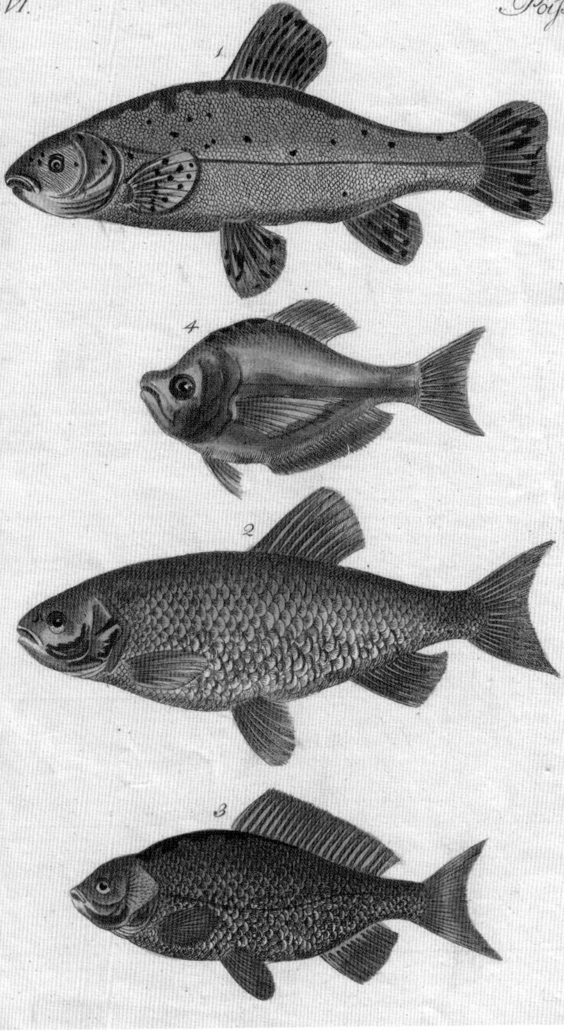
1.
4
2
3

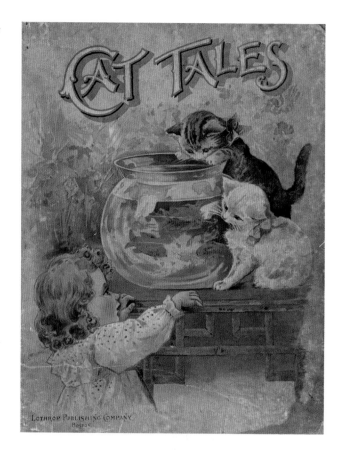

Cover of *Cat Tales: Interesting and Instructive Stories of our Favorite Household Pet* (1893).

daughter of an impoverished Okie tenant farmer in the Dust Bowl of the Great Depression could own one. She is shown on the porch changing the water in the fishbowl among the grime. I wonder what happened to her and her fish.

In 1964 Ford Motor Company even made an advertisement with a child and a goldfish bowl for its new Super Torque Suspension in its sporty Galaxie 500XL line, named to appeal to a public excited about the U.S.–Soviet space race. The advert was placed in magazines like *Ladies' Home Journal*, which were firmly aimed at the American middle class, and featured a little girl holding a goldfish bowl in the front seat of the car which her businessman dad was driving. The copy proclaimed, 'Ford's smooth, silent ride delivers the little girl dry and the goldfish wet.'[81]

Maybe she won the fish at a carnival, for goldfish were not only giveaway promotional items, but prizes at carnivals and fun-fairs in America and the United Kingdom. Unlike in Japan, there

V. Nèlis, 'Toddler and Goldfish', in *Vertel eens wat!* (1905–24).

was no prize for scooping, but rather for tossing a ping-pong ball into a bowl, having a good aim in a coconut shy or success at 'hook-a-duck'. The multiple tries allowed made the chances of victory pretty good, and the image of a child returning from a state fair or funfair holding onto a plastic bag of fish for dear life became iconic in American and British culture.

Little did the lucky winners know that a winsome 2.5-cm (1-in.) fish in a plastic sandwich bag can live up to forty years and grow more than 0.5 m (1.5 ft) long. Tiny 'Nemo' can become a 1.5-kg (3-lb) bruiser. Because so many fairground fish have died from being placed in chlorinated tap water, jumping out of their bowls, overfeeding, filthy water, cats, flushing down the

Front porch of tenant farmer's house near Muskogee, Oklahoma, where the daughter is getting ready to change water in a goldfish bowl; photographed by Russell Lee in July 1939.

toilet and other household misadventures, animal-rights activists and support groups such as the American Society for the Prevention of Cruelty to Animals, the Humane Society of the United States and People for the Ethical Treatment of Animals have called for a ban on the practice. In 2012 English schoolgirl Emily Hirst began a petition – Saving Goldfish Forever – to

Parliament after she herself won a goldfish at an amusement park in Lancashire and was appalled at their living conditions. The petition had 5,942 supporters, including four MPs.[82] Although some county councils have banned the goldfish bowl game, the 2006 Animal Welfare Act in England and Wales remains unchanged. It 'makes it an offence to give away an animal as a prize if the person can reasonably be believed to be under 16 and is not accompanied by an adult [there are some

Goldfish carnival
prize.

144

The iconic Goldfish™ cracker with a smile, created to appeal to children.

exceptions in sections 11(3)–(6) of the Act]'. This means that fish cannot be prevented from being given away as fairground prizes, but that children under sixteen cannot receive them. In 2014 a spokesman for the New York State Fair stated:

We received a number of calls after last year's fair express- ing concern for the well being of these fish after our vendors leave the grounds. Out of an abundance of caution, and in light of the fact that we have a new operator on our Midway, we have decided not to allow them as prizes at [*sic*] this year. We plan to revisit this issue next year.[83]

America and Britain are well behind the Italians in this regard, who passed what they termed an 'avant-garde' law in 2004. The northern Italian city of Monza, known for hosting the Formula 1 Grand Prix, banned goldfish prizes at fairs, as well as outlawing goldfish bowls. Council official Giampietro Mosca was interviewed for an article for ABC News, and stated, 'A fish kept in a bowl has a distorted view of reality . . . and suffers because of this.'[84] Rome quickly followed suit with its own ruling to protect the golden fish. On the other hand, and with due respect to animal rights activists, the oldest known goldfish was a funfair prize for Peter Hand in Yorkshire in 1956. 'Tish' died in 1999, aged 43.[85]

Equally as long-lived and popular with American children is the Goldfish™ cracker made by Pepperidge Farm, now owned by the Campbell Soup Company. These cheese-flavoured nibbles are shaped like tiny fish, and although originally a soup cracker, they are kid-sized, easy for toddlers to pick up and eat. The first Goldfish™ crackers were not American but Swiss, made by biscuit-maker Oscar J. Kambly who was creating a birthday present for his wife. His wife was a Pisces, and he baked her the crackers for love and luck. According to the *Huffington Post*, 'When Pepperidge Farms founder Margaret Rudkin (1897–1967) visited Europe in the 1960s, she was enamored of the adorable crackers and brought them to the United States.'[86]

In 1995 the firm started a campaign that aimed to double its sales and revitalize its soup cracker, giving a proportion of the goldfish a smile and emphasizing nutritional value, noting that Goldfish™ crackers were made of real cheese and whole grains and baked rather than fried.[87] There was a new jingle too, featuring children singing, 'I love the fishes 'cause they're so delicious'. Sales in the U.S. skyrocketed in the first year of the campaign, jumping 25 per cent from 6.8 million to 8.5 million packets.[88] There are now 39 flavours of Goldfish™, including pretzel, parmesan and graham cracker, and the new logo, a cool fish named Finn®, wears sunglasses. There is even a 'Goldfish in Space' cracker, the cartoon fish complete with astronaut's helmet, and the fish crackers interspersed with miniature Saturns and rocket ships. In 1998 Goldfish™ crackers were part of the rations of the crew of the Space Shuttle *Discovery*, who enjoyed making them swim in zero gravity. The 2017 campaign was a contest where children sent in stop-motion films made on iPads and mobile phones featuring the crackers as characters; one of the most popular was 'Goldfish in Space' – goldfish astronauts searching for extraterrestrial life. A trio of teenagers (JChaseFilms) won with *The Wonderful World of Goldfish* featuring a series of vignettes of goldfish crackers mining for diamonds, camping, hot-air ballooning and riding in a train.[89] Their prize, appropriately enough, was a trophy shaped like – you guessed it – a giant orange goldfish cracker.

By the twenty-first century, the goldfish, whether live or baked, had been transformed from exotic rarity to a generic consumer commodity. Its status as a disposable pet and interchangeable

household ornament with a high mortality rate, particularly in families blessed with curious small children, belies its rather higher status in the scientific community for good and for ill. As we will see, goldfish are used as animal models for experiments on cognition, alcoholism and in vision studies, but their ability to breed and thrive when released in the wild presents serious environmental challenges.

5 Goldfish: Villain and Hero

In the comic movie *Goldfish* by Joe Wein (2007), two schoolgirls named Suzy and Jenny 'save' classroom goldfish by flushing them down the toilet in the belief that all drains lead to the ocean (a cultural reference to the Disney film *Finding Nemo*). Their action of disposing of the goldfish to get them back 'home' is culturally representative of the unforeseen development of the environmental repercussions of keeping goldfish as pets. We have seen in this book that goldfish are ambiguous, shown to be common and rare, but in their impact on the ecosystem and on scientific discovery they are also self-contradictory, Jekyll and Hyde, villain and hero.

Goldfish that are flushed down the toilet, escape from ornamental ponds, or are dumped in lakes when fishermen use them as bait can interbreed with common carp, multiplying and disrupting the ecosystem, achieving a density of up to 17,000 fish per hectare, not surprising considering a female produces 40,000 eggs per year.[1] They are voracious and opportunistic omnivores. Because goldfish have no stomach, they cannot store food well, and so graze during the day on plants, small snails, insects and crustaceans. They decimate native frog populations by eating tadpoles and snacking on the eggs and larvae of long-toed salamanders, making them of prime concern to conservationists. Goldfish also defecate – a lot – which causes algal and plankton growth, and as they uproot vegetation when they feed on the muddy bottoms of lakes, they increase water turbidity. Rooting at the bottom also destroys feeding and refuge habitats of other fish.[2] In 2016 *Carassius auratus* was listed as an aquatic nuisance species in six states: Colorado, Nevada, New York, North Carolina, Oregon and Pennsylvania.[3] Goldfish can be villains, and there is good reason why a group of goldfish is known as a 'troubling'.

In 2015 more than 3,000 goldfish took over Teller Lake in Boulder, Colorado, after someone dumped a handful of their unwanted pets. The invasion made international news and even featured on Comedy Central's *@midnight* programme. Host Chris Hardwick called it a 'revolutionary goldfish ****fest', noting 'these guys are really making the most out of not dying in a toilet. Good for them.'[4]

On last report, the Fisheries Commission planned to electro-shock the goldfish to get them to float to the surface, and then donate them to a raptor rehabilitation centre as feed. In 2012 the goldfish's cousin, the koi carp, was removed from Thunderbird Lake in Boulder by a similar process of 'electro-fishing', resulting in 2,275 dead fish and some very happy eagles.[5] But the planned execution at Teller Lake never took place because Mother Nature intervened with a flock of hungry American white pelicans, whose summer and migratory range encompasses much of the American West. The pelicans saw the bright fish as they flew overhead and gobbled thousands in a few weeks. Colorado Parks and Wildlife is thinking about 'strategic placement of rehabilitated pelicans' if the problem occurs again.[6] In a draft regulation of 2017, the State of Colorado also considered removing goldfish from the list of species of acceptable bait for bass fisherman.[7] The goldfish can escape from the hook, and fishermen sometimes empty their bait bucket in the lake to save having to take it home, an odoriferous business in an enclosed car.

The goldfish gobbler: a heron taking advantage of a goldfish invasion of a pond.

Thunderbird and Teller lakes are only two of the more recent environmental catastrophes caused by rogue goldfish. Researchers at the University of Nevada, Reno, found that they have also invaded the popular ski resort and tourist destination of Lake Tahoe, growing up to a foot and a half long.[8] A similar phenomenon has occurred within the Don River watershed in Toronto's waterways, the River Vasse in southwestern Australia, and in Alberta, which in 2015 started a 'Don't Let it Loose' campaign. One reason for their spread is the large distances they swim, some up to 225 km (140 mi.) per year, and they migrate to spawn, just like the wild carp. Using passive acoustic telemetry, researchers found that goldfish in a southwestern Australian river travelled 'a mean of 0.30 km (linear river kilometres) per day within the array, and one fish moved 231.3 km over the 365-day study period (including 5.4 km in a 24 hr period)'.[9] Invaders on the move, these infringing fish.

On the other hand, goldfish are heroes to science, and sometimes long-suffering ones. Typing the term 'goldfish' into the

Goldfish can grow to be more than 40 cm (16 in.) long and weigh more than 2.5 kg (6 lb). They are classified as an invasive species in California.

Bodleian Library database reveals over 40,000 scientific papers devoted to goldfish studies. In their sensory organs, goldfish are a lot like us, making them ideal experimental models that are cheap and easily obtainable. They are smart enough to be trainable in studies in visual perception and cognition, as they perceive the same colours as humans. Their skin is analogous to ours as well. Just like us, their skin pigment cells or chromatophores produce pigment in response to light, so they can get a tan; maybe that is why the Goldfish™ cracker logo has to wear sunglasses.

The fish also can turn white if left long enough in a darkened room, making them suited to analysis of the effects of sun exposure on skin cancer rates. The water turbidity that goldfish generate due to feeding goes hand in hand with their incredible ability to taste, the roof of their mouth and whiskers having thousands of tastebuds to guide them efficiently to a meal in muddy water.[10] Because goldfish are omnivores, they wisely taste their food before it is chewed by their teeth at the back of their mouths, and stones are quickly spat out. These super-tasting abilities make the goldfish gustatory system useful, particularly as the chemistry of taste signalling in fish is, again, similar to that in higher mammals such as humans.

Armstrong & Hess, 'Helitrim Trimming Potentiometer with a Goldfish' (1960–69). This photograph is part of a series of marketing images used to demonstrate the small size of Helipot potentiometers. Potentiometers regulate the flow of electricity, like the volume dial on a radio.

Goldfish as experimental models in fact have had an extensive history, particularly in detecting levels of toxicity, whether in pharmaceuticals or in the environment. The classic paper on goldfish as test animals was a study of the toxicity levels of digitalis, performed by Paul S. Pittenger and Charles E. Vanderkleed (1915).[11] Digitalis extracted from the purple foxglove increases the intensity of contractions of the heart muscle, but diminishes their rate, a property discovered in 1775 by Scottish physician William Withering (1741–1799). Although several botanists including John Ray knew of its poisonous qualities, noting that in humoral medicine it 'is proper only for strong constitutions, as it purges very violently, and excites excessive vomiting', and it had been used to treat scrofula (lymphatic tuberculosis), it was not until Withering that its specific cardiac properties were known and applied.[12] Withering wrote:

In the year 1775, my opinion was asked concerning a family receipt . . . I was told it had long been kept a secret by an old woman in Shropshire . . . that the effects produced were violent vomiting and purging . . . The medicine was composed of twenty or more different herbs; but it was not very difficult for one conversant in these subjects, to perceive, that the active herb could be no other than the Foxglove.[13]

He used it as a diuretic to treat dropsy (oedema), a side effect of congestive heart failure. Several luminaries were treated with it for heart conditions, including Vincent van Gogh, but there were a few issues with the drug. Like many botanical medicines, the active ingredients are a mixture of different molecules (cardiac glycosides and saponins), and the concentration of them differs in strength with the growing season of the plant. The therapeutic dose of digitalis is also very small, so it is very easy to exceed a safe dosage, leading to patient fatality. Hence an experimental model was sought that could produce accurate levels of toxicity, and the goldfish seemed a good choice.

It was thought that frogs and guinea pigs had too great a variation in absorption rates of digitalis to be used in the standardization of drugs, but goldfish seemed ideal. As Pittenger noted at a 1919 scientific conference in New York,

> the great absorptive power of the gills of a fish, together with the fact that they contain a large number of blood vessels through which the blood circulates direct from the heart, made this animal present itself as a possible means of eliminating these variations due to absorption.[14]

Trials with several thousand goldfish showed they were also sensitive to 2.5 per cent variations of the 'strength of the dilutions of the digitalis in which they are placed'; the assay was relatively simple and goldfish could be 'purchased wholesale for from 45 to 60 cents per dozen . . . at all seasons of the year'.[15]

The success with the Pittenger-Vanderkleed 'goldfish method' subsequently led the fish to be tested with a huge variety of different substances in a major study done at the University of Illinois in 1917 led by Edwin Powers. Goldfish were placed in tanks containing different concentrations of toxic salts, including lithium chloride (used to treat bipolar disorder since the 1870s), barium chloride (used in the hardening of steel and highly toxic) and cadmium chloride (used in the oil paint cadmium yellow), as well as other substances including potassium cyanide. It was found that there was a direct relationship between fish mortality and concentration of the solution of the toxic substance, with a threshold level of toxicity. Goldfish were subsequently transformed into the canaries in the mine, and as there was no Davy safety lamp to replace them, they have been used to test everything from growth hormones to DDT and other mosquito-control insecticides to sexual stimulants.

Their ubiquity in scientific research eventually led to the realization in 1968 by Ralph Ryback at Harvard Medical School that goldfish were even excellent animal models with which to study alcoholism, as their blood alcohol levels 'come into equilibrium with the alcohol solution in which the fish swim within 6 hours'.[16] That means its blood alcohol level can be ascertained by simply measuring the water alcohol concentration. For example, goldfish were subjected to tests of their memory and ability to negotiate new environments in a simple Y-shaped maze after being exposed to different concentrations and types of alcoholic beverages. Fish with bourbon in the water learned more poorly than fish swimming in ethanol, due to the presence of congeners in bourbon such as fusel oil, organic acids, esters and aldehydes, which give it its taste. Humans drinking bourbon versus those sticking to vodka, which has low levels of congeners, have similar results.[17] After continuous exposure to alcohol, the goldfish's ability to learn was unaffected by higher levels in the water, and so, like humans, goldfish develop alcohol tolerance.

It was recently discovered that goldfish, unlike humans, have an alternative metabolic pathway to make alcohol when they are in a low-oxygen environment. When humans do not have enough oxygen, we switch into anaerobic respiration to break down glucose to produce energy, the by-product lactic acid; in runners, this build-up is why leg muscles can burn, and the process cannot be sustained for long. Due to a mutation that took place 8 million years ago, goldfish have a separately evolved metabolic pathway. Rather than make lactic acid as a by-product of metabolism in a low-oxygen environment, such as the bottom of a frozen lake or pond, they make ethanol and expel the excess booze from their gills. This neat metabolic trick allows them to survive harsh winters, and contributes to their hardiness and their ability to outcompete other species. Impressive, though there has to be an easier way of making whisky. As goldfish are naturally exposed to higher ethanol concentrations in their muscle tissue, researchers at the universities of Oslo and Liverpool who performed the study noted that they hold promise as 'model systems for the study of molecular mechanism protecting against chronic ethanol exposure'.[18] In other words, goldfish may hold the key to mitigating adverse effects of chronic alcoholism, particularly as they spend the winters with a blood alcohol level that exceeds drunk-driving limits.

Not only are goldfish their own distillers, but their optic nerve can regrow and regenerate after being crushed, preserving vision. Nerve cells in goldfish retinas are similar to stem cells in humans in that they are regenerative and have a type of plasticity so they can develop into different types of more specialized cells as needed. Proteins in the nerves of goldfish that can regenerate are also similar in proteins in mammalian nerves that are made during nerve formation and growth.[19] Studies of the molecular mechanisms of the regeneration of goldfish nerves thus give scientists a better understanding of how nerve tissue in higher vertebrates, like humans, could be made to regenerate with new molecular drugs. This means developing not only ways of restoring vision, but methods of restoring neural function in cases of paralysis.

Goldfish were key animals in early experiments to understand the role of neuropeptides and the action of drugs. Leading twentieth-century pharmacologist J. H. Gaddum conducted a series of experiments where he used a short piece of goldfish intestine, placed in a warm oxygenated salt solution to keep it alive, to study the effects of drugs on the longitudinal muscle of the gut. Previous experiments using intestines of other creatures were some of the first to show the action of adrenaline on living tissue – making the gut contract. The relative contraction and stimulation of an isolated piece of goldfish small intestine was used to detect and measure a new substance discovered by Gaddum in 1931, a polypeptide called Substance P, which is found in the grey matter of mammalian brains. Subsequent work showed that Substance P is a key substance produced in response to environmental stress, causing dilation of blood vessels, increased cell growth and multiplication, and the transmission of pain information to the central nervous system. It seems to have tremendous importance for the development of pain relievers, and has even been linked to mood disorder and male aggression.

Goldfish feeding
from the hand.

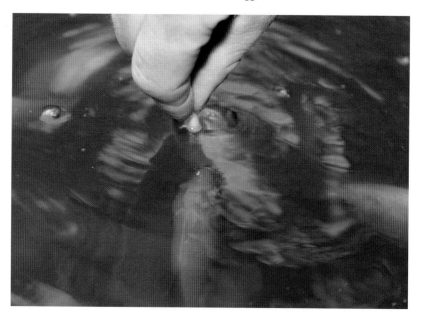

As we use goldfish and their organs as experimental models so extensively, it may be discomfiting to realize that they exhibit intelligence. It has long been known anecdotally that goldfish seem to be more active in anticipation of feeding time, but it appears that there is more to it than instinct. Philip Gee, David Stephenson and Donald Wright, psychologists at the University of Plymouth, discovered that goldfish can learn to press a lever at a particular time of day to obtain food, clustering around the lever for the hour it is operated.[20] When the food dispensers were made inactive for six days, the fish still remembered mealtime for two days, and then stopped pressing the lever. When the lever was reactivated with food, the fish quickly pressed the lever at the appropriate time. A decoy feeder that never dispensed food did not fool them either. Other studies have shown that they can associate sounds with feeding, though they do not drool in a Pavlovian response to the sound of a bell. Israeli scientists played a particular sound at feeding time before the fish were released into the wild for several months. On their return, the sound was played again, and the fish gathered at their feeding place. Goldfish can tell time, and they can remember through associative learning.

Do you wonder why goldfish respond to sound, not only to obtain food, but to swim away when you tap on the glass of their aquarium? Sensory organs along their flanks (called lateral lines) detect sounds as vibrations. These organs communicate to a single pair of brain cells (called Mauthner cells), which in turn trigger 'muscle contractions along one side of the body, directing the fish away from the sound'.[21] Disabling these organs affects the fishes' ability to move away from the sound. Blindfolding the fish on the other hand does not affect their behaviour, so vision is not involved in their swimming away. I am trying to imagine the process of blindfolding a goldfish. It is probably easier to avoid tapping on the glass.

Goldfish can also be trained to perform more complex tasks. In the 1970s it was shown that 'Fish can display quite sophisticated thermoregulatory behaviour . . . when goldfish trained to control water heaters by lever-pressing [they] were able to regulate the temperature to within 1°C.'[22] It is claimed that Chinese goldfish keepers can train their pets to feed out of their hands, and through operative conditioning they can push miniature footballs and swim through tunnels and hoops. Goldfish can even recognize shapes. In 2011, experiments by Caroline DeLong at Rochester Institute of Technology showed that goldfish could recognize shapes, in particular a black circle attached to the tank. A goldfish named Poseidon would choose that circle even when other shapes such as rectangles were present.[23] Poseidon would tap the circle with her mouth to receive food. Recent results from the DeLong laboratory using a similar experimental procedure indicate that goldfish can do numbers too: 'fish given extensive training can achieve accuracy (>90%) on a numerical task comparable to well-trained birds, humans, or non-human primates'.[24] Instead of shapes, the fish were exposed to arrays of varying numbers of black dots on white backgrounds to see if they could discriminate between numerical quantities. It is thought such learned behaviour helps the fish to optimize foraging because they can compare the numbers of prey in two different areas of their habitat.

It seems the goldfish is ubiquitous, with ambiguous status in its relationship to humans: at times a troubling environmental nuisance that stirs up the waters, at others a useful experimental model; sometimes of little value, a carnival prize, while elsewhere it is considered an uncomfortably smart little creature demonstrating incredible evolutionary adaptation to its habitat.

The fish is an oxymoron not just in the sciences but also in the arts, with the capacity to bring great luck or terrible tragedy.

In 1833 Alexander Pushkin wrote the fairy tale *The Fisherman and the Fish*, the Brothers Grimm his inspiration. For Pushkin, the goldfish was liminal, a hero and a villain all at once.

The story ran like this. Once upon a time, a peasant living in a mud hut eked out a living as a fisherman, his wife spinning cloth. Fishing in a calm sea, he caught a very small and vulnerable goldfish struggling in his net. Much to his surprise, the little fish spoke in a high, frightened voice, begging for her freedom in return for a reward. The fisherman let the fish go, and said kindly, 'God bless you, golden fish. I don't need anything from you . . . swim free, swim where you wish.'

When he told his wife about the strange encounter, she was incensed, and cursed, 'Simple fool, fool of a simpleton', reminding

Detail no. 6 from a 19th-century illustrated tale by Aleksander Pushkin, *Skazka o rybake i rybke* (Tale of the Fisherman and the Fish).

her husband, 'You could have at least asked her for a watering trough, because ours is broken.' The old man with some trepidation went back to the shore and approached the fish and bowed, apologizing for his demanding wife. The fish comforted him, and promised to grant his wish. The trough appeared, and the sea grew more disturbed. The wife's demands incrementally escalated to a new frying pan and a new house, and when the goldfish's gift of a pleasant whitewashed little cottage was not good enough, she demanded to be a noblewoman, and then a mighty *tsarina* with a sable jacket and pearls and fine red boots. Sitting on her throne and surrounded by servants, she banished her fisherman husband to live in the stable. The sea grew ever more stormy, the sky dark and troubled. Finally, his recently ennobled wife, increasingly insane with power, made her last request – to be Empress of All Land and Sea. Now, thunder and lightning and giant waves crashed on the shore, and the fisherman had to yell above the noise to make his request of the little fish. This time she made no reply but simply turned and swam away. The fisherman returned home to find his mud hut, his poor wife sitting outside it and a broken trough.

Soviet Union stamp commemorating Pushkin's tale, 1975.

The story, like so many of Pushkin's works, had an alternative meaning. According to Robert Chandler,

It seems odd that Pushkin's old woman should see ruling over the sea as a higher destiny than that of being 'a mighty tsaritsa'. Professor Olga Meerson, however, has pointed out to me that Catherine the Great was eager to rule over the Black Sea; between 1768 and 1792 she fought two wars against Turkey in order to achieve this. And Catherine, like Pushkin's old woman, had usurped her husband's place; she had deposed her husband Peter III in 1762, before these wars. In reality Catherine was generous to her favourite

Harold C. Harvey (1874–1941), *Laura and Paul Jewill Hill*, 1915, oil painting. One can see how the artist was inspired by Van Eyck's *Arnolfini Portrait*, the mirror reflecting the other people in the room, including presumably the artist.

Prince Potyomkin and her subsequent lovers, but there is no doubt that Pushkin saw her as having treated her male favourites abusively.[25]

Catherine's behaviour with her favourites was much like that of the fisherman's wife with her husband, and much like we treat the goldfish sometimes. The Bosnians have another, more morally uplifting, version, a story of a poor woman who caught a goldfish, released it and in return was rewarded with happiness and wealth.

Even when they are considered a common household pet, goldfish have become the subject of fantasy and comedic films exploring their keeping as a childhood ritual. In some cases, as goldfish were global travellers themselves, they become symbols for the often-ambiguous boundaries of race and cultural identity endemic to globalization. In the film *Goldfish Go Home* (*Akane Iro No Yakusoku: Sanba da kingyo*) by Shôhei Shiozaki (2012), Ricardo, a Brazilian boy of Japanese descent, comes to Japan because his parents want to work in a goldfish-breeding village (Yamatokōriyama City in Nara Prefecture). The boy is ostracized due to his place of birth, bullied at school and longs to return to Brazil. One day, however, the outsider discovers a goldfish shining in blue in an ancient tomb. He tries to solve this mysterious sighting with Hanako, a Japanese classmate whose father is a goldfish breeder. The boy and girl protect the blue goldfish (who turns out to be the spirit of a Chinese princess) from the mayor and other adults who try to profit from her until an ancient legend of goldfish triggers a miracle in the town. Ricardo, like the goldfish, is redeemed and revered due to his liminal and shifting status on the periphery.

In the Japanese animated fantasy *Ponyo* (*Gake no ue no Ponyo*, 2008), released in the u.s. and Canada in a dubbed English version by Disney, the goldfish is not assisted by humans, but becomes one herself. In an ichthyologic rendition of *Pinocchio*, Ponyo is a red-haired goldfish (the Disney adaptation of a redcap oranda) who wants to become a human after falling in love with a five-year-old boy named Sōsuke, who saves her from suffocating when she swims into a jar. Sōsuke cuts his finger when he breaks the jar to release her, and Ponyo licks it, healing it instantly.

Much like Pushkin's goldfish, Ponyo is no ordinary fish, but a goldfish princess whose real name is Brunhilde, the daughter of a wizard, Fujimoto, and Granmamare, the goddess of mercy. By tasting human blood, Ponyo uses magic to become human to be with Sōsuke, but by doing so, she unknowingly unleashes environmental catastrophe. The moon falls out of its orbit and the ocean swells in a giant tsunami, symptoms of terrible natural imbalance. The merciful Granmamare decides that if Sōsuke can prove his

Large goldfish in Carroll Creek, Frederick, Maryland.

love for Ponyo, she can live as a human, but if he fails, she will be transformed into sea foam. In the course of events in the film, Ponyo turns back into a fish due to overuse of her magic, and Granmamare asks Sōsuke if he can love her whether fish or human. He simply says he 'loves all the Ponyos' and, passing the test, is reunited with his love, now human, and natural balance is restored.

This film and its sweet magic are also a parable, it seems, for our relationship with our own Ponyos. Through their habitation with us, goldfish have innocently unleashed environmental catastrophe, but only because we have treated them as a disposable commodity, or used them as cheap bait, without recognizing their true value and role in the natural world. Perhaps when we see their magical qualities, of beauty and grace, of evolutionary adaptation and of intelligence, we can respect *Carassius auratus* in its own right. We can love all the Ponyos.

FIN.

Timeline of the Goldfish

265–420	960	1163	1368–1644

Reports of golden and red fish in Chinese Jin dynasty

References to goldfish in works of Song dynasty

Beginning of crossbreeding in the goldfish pond at Te Shou Palace in Hangzhou

Development of goldfish bowls in the Ming dynasty and multicoloured fish

1810	1878	1880–83	1912

Beginning of *kingyo sukui*, or goldfish scooping games, in Japan

Free goldfish offered to American citizens by the United States Commission of Fish and Fisheries

Development in America of the comet goldfish

The Goldfish painted by Henri Matisse, representative to him of tranquillity of mind

1994	2006	2007	2008

Phil Gee, David Stephenson and Donald Wright, psychologists at the University of Plymouth, discover that goldfish can associate feeding with a given task, such as pressing a level. Goldfish also associate feeding with a time of the day

Giving away goldfish at funfairs made illegal in Britain

Goldfish film by Joe Wein released, shot in an elementary school during school holidays

Animated film *Ponyo* released by Walt Disney, winner of the annual Japan Animation Prize

17TH CENTURY	1711	1755	1758–9

Introduction of goldfish to Japan during the Edo period (1615–24), and development of ryukin varieties

James Petiver's drawing of goldfish, the first known in England

Introduction of goldfish to France

Carl Linnaeus (1707–1778), the founder of binomial taxonomy, gives the goldfish its modern moniker, *Carassius auratus*

1914	1939	1951	1962

Joseph E. Bausman awarded the first prize for best fish bred from the Aquarium Society of Philadelphia

Goldfish-swallowing contest craze starts in the United States by Lothrop Withington Jr

William Hanna and Joseph Barbera introduce the cartoon character Goldfish in the *Tom and Jerry* cartoon, 'Jerry and the Goldfish'. The character later appears in another cartoon short, 'Filet Meow'

Introduction of Pepperidge Farm Goldfish™ crackers to America

2015	2016	2017

Goldfish invasion of Teller Lake, Colorado

First evidence of spawning migration by goldfish

In England, an aquarium worker named Derek makes a 'wheelchair harness' for his goldfish that suffers from air bladder problems and cannot swim properly

References

1 NO NEED TO CARP: THE ORIGINS AND ANATOMY OF A GOLDFISH

1 The oldest domesticated fish in the world is the wild common carp
(*Cyprinus carpio* L), cultivated in fishponds 2,000 years ago by
the ancient Romans. E. K. Balon, 'About the Oldest Domesticates
Among Fishes', *Journal of Fish Biology*, 65 (2004), pp. 1–27,
p. 2. For an altogether more beautiful and serious rendition
of reincarnation as a goldfish that inspired this paragraph, see
David Hernandez, 'The Goldfish', *Iowa Review*, XXXIV/2 (2004),
p. 84.

2 Pierre Schneider, *Matisse*, trans. Michael Taylor and Bridget
Strevens Romer (London, 1984), p. 43.

3 Joseph Smartt, *Goldfish Varieties and Genetics: A Handbook for
Breeders* (Oxford, 2008), p. 1.

4 Ibid., p. 2.

5 See 'Linnaeus' Garden', www2.linnaeus.uu.se, accessed 15 January
2018; 'Letter from Job Baster to Carl Linnaeus, 1 September 1763,
letter L3300', http://linnaeus.c18.net.

6 Håkan Olsén and Ingvar Svanberg, 'Introduction', in *Historical
Aquaculture in Northern Europe*, ed. Madeleine Bonow, Håkan Olsén
and Ingvar Svanberg (Huddinge, 2016), p. 15. See 'Letter from Pehr
af Bjerkén to Carl Linnaeus, 7 October 1759, letter L2603', http://
linnaeus.c18.net.

7 Christopher Appelt and Peter Sorensen, 'Female Goldfish Signal
Spawning Readiness by Altering When and Where they Release
a Urinary Pheromone', *Animal Behaviour*, 74 (2007), pp. 1329–38.

8 Robert Crosby, 'Understanding the Environmental and Hormonal Control of Goldfish Reproduction', *Goldfish Report* (July/August 2004), p. 8, www.goldfishsociety.org.

9 See 'How to Make Your Own Spawning Mop', *Practical Fishkeeping*, www.practicalfishkeeping.co.uk, 13 June 2016.

10 M. Charbonnier, 'On the Reproduction and Development of the Telescope Fish of China', *Annals and Magazine of Natural History*, XI/61 (1873), pp. 76–7.

11 Hugo Mulertt, *The Goldfish and its Systematic Culture* (New York, 1910), p. 25. This point was made by Hugh M. Smith, 'Goldfish and their Cultivation in America', *National Geographic*, XLVI/4 (1924), p. 382.

12 Balon, 'Oldest Domesticates Among Fishes', p. 14.

13 Shu-Yan Wang et al., 'Origin of Chinese Goldfish and Sequential Loss of Genetic Diversity Accompanies New Breeds', *PLOS ONE*, VIII/3 (2013), p. e59571.

14 Jing Wang et al., 'Evidence for the Evolutionary Origin of Goldfish derived from the Distant Crossing of Red Crucian Carp x Common Carp', *BMC Genetics*, XV/33 (2014), https://bmcgenet.biomedcentral.com, accessed 5 March 2018.

15 Balon, 'Oldest Domesticates Among Fishes', p. 15.

16 George F. Hervey and Jack Hems, *The Goldfish* (London, 1981), p. 33.

17 Miles J. G. Parsons et al., 'Fish Choruses off Port Hedland, Western Australia', *Journal of Bioacoustics: The International Journal of Animal Sound and its Recording*, XXVI/2 (2017), pp. 135–52.

18 Balon, 'Oldest Domesticates Among Fishes', p. 17.

19 Edme-Louis Billardon de Sauvigny, *Histoire naturelle des dorades de la Chine* (Paris, 1780), p. 21.

20 Shisan C. Chen, 'A History of the Domestication and the Factors of the Varietal Formation of the Common Goldfish, *Carassius Auratus*', *Scientia Sinica*, V/1–4 (1956), p. 291.

21 Smartt, *Goldfish Varieties*, p. 13.

22 Mu Chu, *Beauties of the Earth*, 1239, woodcut edition.

23 Chi-cheng Chen, *The Topography of Chincheng*, 1223, woodcut edition of the Sung family of Linhai in the Chia Ching reign.

24 Chen, 'A History of the Domestication', p. 297.

25 Tim Matson, *Earth Ponds: The Country Pond Maker's Guide to Building, Maintenance, and Restoration* (New York, 2012), p. 13.

26 Chen, 'A History of the Domestication', p. 294.

27 Harriet Sherwood, 'Why Buddhist "fangsheng" Mercy Release Rituals can be More Cruel than Kind', www.theguardian.com, 25 September 2017; Debra West, 'Buddhists Release Animals, Dismaying Wildlife Experts', www.nytimes.com, 11 January 1997.

28 The Environment and Animal Society of Taiwan (EAST) has campaigned against Buddhist mercy release. See www.east.org.tw; Steven Crook, *Taiwan* (Guilford, CT, 2014), pp. 10–11.

29 Regina Krahl, 'Fishes in the Imperial Bowl: An Exceptional Xuande Bowl', www.sothebys.com, 27 March 2017.

30 Lao Ning, 'Goldfish, a Feast for the Eye', www.chinadaily.com.cn, 5 March 1991.

31 Mark Edward Lewis, *China's Cosmopolitan Empire: The Tang Dynasty* (Cambridge, MA, 2009), p. 4.

32 Jonathan DeHart, 'Goldfish: From Tang Dynasty Ponds to 21st Century Aquariums', https://thediplomat.com, 9 October 2013.

33 John W. Chaffee, *Branches of Heaven: A History of the Imperial Clan of Sung China* (Cambridge, MA, 1999), pp. 144–5.

34 Ibid., p. 180.

35 Smartt, *Goldfish Varieties*, p. 14.

36 Chen, 'A History of the Domestication', p. 299.

37 Smartt, *Goldfish Varieties*, p. 16.

38 Ibid.

39 Balon, 'Oldest Domesticates Among Fishes', p. 17.

40 Chen, 'A History of the Domestication', p. 299.

41 Hervey and Hems, *The Goldfish*, p. 84.

42 Ibid., p. 47.

43 Smartt, *Goldfish Varieties*, p. 118.

44 Ibid., p. 117. A new table (January 2014) in even more detail has been jointly produced by the Bristol Aquarists' Society, the GFSA and the Goldfish Society of Great Britain, www.bristol-aquarists. org.uk, accessed 10 February 2018.

45 See 'Background Information about Goldfish',
    www.bristol-aquarists.org.uk, accessed 10 February 2018.
46 Ibid.
47 Hervey and Hems, *The Goldfish*, p. 84.
48 Smartt, *Goldfish Varieties*, p. 6.
49 Ibid., pp. 6–7.
50 'Background Information about Goldfish', www.bristol-aquarists.
    org.uk.
51 Bernd Brunner, *The Ocean at Home: An Illustrated History of the
    Aquarium* (London, 2005), p. 24.
52 Victoria Charles, *Chinese Porcelain* (New York, 2011), p. 156.
53 Ibid., p. 158.
54 'Stemcup 1426–36', http://collections.vam.ac.uk, accessed
    25 March 2018.
55 'Ming Bowl', www.ngv.vic.gov.au, accessed 10 February 2018.
56 Justin Crozier, 'A Unique Experiment', *China in Focus: The Journal
    of the Society for Anglo-Chinese Understanding*, 12 (June 2002),
    www.sacu.org.
57 Louise A. Cort and Jan Stewart, *Joined Colors: Decoration and
    Meaning in Chinese Porcelain* (Washington, DC, 1993), p. 5.
58 Brunner, *The Ocean at Home*, p. 24.
59 V. Huckstorf and J. Freyhof, '*Carassius auratus*', the IUCN Red List
    of Threatened Species 2013: e.T166083A1110472. www.iucnredlist.
    org, accessed 10 February 2018.

2 THE JAPANESE GOLDFISH

1 Engelbert Kaempfer, *The History of Japan: Together with a
   Description of the Kingdom of Siam 1690–92*, vol. II (Glasgow, 1906),
   pp. 325–6.
2 'Engelbert Kaempfer: The History of Japan (1727)',
   www.eisenbibliothek.ch, accessed 22 February 2018.
3 Sakeda Masatoshi and George Akita, 'The Samurai Disestablished:
   Abei Iwane and His Stipend', *Monumenta Nipponica*, XLI/3
   (Autumn 1986), pp. 299–330.

4 Harry D. Harootunian, 'The Economic Rehabilitation of the Samurai in the Early Meiji Period', *Journal of Asian Studies*, XIX/4 (August 1960), pp. 433–44. See also Yoshiichi Matsui, Takayoshi Kumagai and L. C. Betts, *Goldfish Guide* (Neptune, NJ, 1991), p. 25.

5 'Past and Present: The History of Goldfish', www.city. yamatokoriyama.nara.jp, accessed 3 March 2018.

6 'Text accompanying Goldfish Vendor, 1800s by Katsushika Hokusai', https://collections.artsmia.org, accessed 3 March 2018.

7 Hugh Smith, *Japanese Goldfish: Their Varieties and Cultivation* (Washington, DC, 1909), p. 10.

8 Ibid., p. 46.

9 Luís Fróis, S. J., *The First European Description of Japan, 1585: A Critical English-language Edition of Striking Contrasts in the Customs of Europe and Japan*, trans. and annotated Richard K. Danford, Robin D. Gill and Daniel T. Reff, with a critical introduction by Daniel T. Reff (New York, 2014), p. 89.

10 Helen Merritt and Nanako Yamada, *Woodblock Kuchi-e Prints: Reflections of Meiji Culture* (Honolulu, HI, 2000), p. 216.

11 'Past and Present: The History of Goldfish', www.city. yamatokoriyama.nara.jp.

12 'Goldfish Scooping', https://wikivisually.com, accessed 3 March 2018.

13 'Enthusiast Teaches Japanese Art of Goldfish Scooping', www.japantimes.co.jp, 23 June 2016.

14 'To Be Exactly the Same Over and Over Again – Repetition in Art', www.widewalls.ch, 24 August 2016.

15 Johnny, 'Riusuke Fukahori: Goldfish Salvation', www.spoon-tamago.com, 10 January 2012.

16 Johnny, 'Goldfish Bubble Wrap by Daisuke Akiyama', www.spoon-tamago.com, 20 July 2014.

17 'Goldfish Poop Gang', http://tvtropes.org, accessed 16 February 2018.

18 Chunichi Shimbun, 'Young Goldfish Breeders Rise to Challenge in Aichi', www.japantimes.co.jp, 26 May 2012.

19 Shinnosuke Matsubara, 'Goldfish and their Culture in Japan', *Bulletin of the Bureau of Fisheries*, 28 (1908), p. 383.

20 Kazuya Takaoka and Sachiko Kuru, *Kingyo: The Artistry of Japanese Goldfish* (Tokyo, New York and London, 2003), p. 344.

21 Ibid.

22 'Oranda Goldfish', http://animal-world.com, accessed 19 February 2018.

23 Takaoka and Kuru, *Kingyo*, p. 345.

24 'Memory of the Netherlands: 'Journey to the Court', www.geheugenvannederland.nl, accessed 19 February 2018.

25 The lists of Japanese demands from 1823 from the Nationaal Archief in the Netherlands are digitized at the Memory of the Netherlands site, www.geheugenvannederland.nl/en, accessed 19 February 2018.

26 'Ranchu: King of Goldfish', www.practicalfishkeeping.co.uk, 13 June 2016.

27 Takaoka and Kuru, *Kingyo*, p. 351.

28 Smith, *Japanese Goldfish*, p. 24.

29 Ibid., p. 25.

30 Takaoka and Kuru, *Kingyo*, p. 346.

3 THE ENGLISH AND EUROPEAN GOLDFISH, 1500–1800

1 Joseph Smartt, *Goldfish Varieties and Genetics: A Handbook for Breeders* (Oxford, 2008), p. 25.

2 See www.pepysdiary.com, 28 May 1665 and 19 August 1664.

3 Caroline Grigson, *Menagerie: The History of Exotic Animals in England, 1100–1837* (Oxford, 2016), p. 37.

4 James Petiver, *Gazophylacium Naturae et Artis*, in *Opuscula Petiveriana* (London, 1695–1717), p. 8.

5 John Henry Gray, *China: A History of the Laws, Manners, and Customs of the People* (New York, 1898), p. 202.

6 Lucy Peltz, 'Sutton Nicholls (fl. 1680–1740)', www.oxforddnb.com, accessed 20 February 2018.

7   D. E. Allen, 'Petiver, James (*c.* 1665–1718)', www.oxforddnb.com, accessed 20 February 2018.

8   John Ray, 'Letter to Edward Lhwyd, 11 June 1701', http://emlo. bodleian.ox.ac.uk, accessed 20 February 2018. For another view of Ray's comment, see K. A. James, '"Humbly Dedicated": Petiver and the Audience for Natural History in Early Eighteenth-century Britain', *Archives of Natural History*, XXXI/2 (2004), p. 320.

9   J. M. Camarasa and N. Ibáñez, 'Joan Salvador and James Petiver: A Scientific Correspondence (1706–14) in Time of War', *Archives of Natural History*, XXXIV/1 (2007), pp. 140–73.

10 Allen, 'Petiver, James (*c.* 1665–1718)'.

11 Thomas Hearne, *Remarks and Collections of Thomas Hearne*, vol. VI (Oxford, 1902), p. 255. Hearne remarked in his diary entry of 4 December 1718: 'Sloane has purchased the Library of the late Mr Petiver, Apothecary in Aldersgate Street, for 4000 Pounds'. For a catalogue of the Sloane Herbarium, which contains Petiver's specimens, see www.nhm.ac.uk, accessed 20 February 2018.

12 See Anne Goldgar, *Impolite Learning: Conduct and Community in the Republic of Letters, 1680–1750* (New Haven, CT, 1995).

13 Giovanni Aloi, *Speculative Taxidermy: Natural History, Animal Surfaces and Art in the Anthropocene* (New York, 2018), p. 58.

14 Sebastian Kroupa, '*Ex epistulis Philippinensibus:* George Joseph Kamel SJ and His Correspondence Network', *Centaurus*, LVII/4 (2015), pp. 229–30.

15 C. E. Jarvis and P. H. Oswald, 'The Collecting Activities of James Cuninghame FRS on the Voyage of *Tuscan* to China (Amoy) between 1697 and 1699', *Notes and Records: The Royal Society Journal of the History of Science*, LXIX/2 (June 2015), pp. 135–53.

16 Kroupa, *Ex epistulis*, p. 236.

17 George Edwards, *Natural History of Uncommon Birds and of Some Other Rare and Undescribed Animals* (London, 1743–51), preface.

18 Arthur MacGregor, 'Patrons and Collectors: Contributors of Zoological Subjects to the Works of George Edwards (1694–1773)',

Journal of the History of Collections, XXVI/1 (1 March 2014), pp. 35–44, quote from article abstract.

19 Worth died in August 1741, succeeded by Captain Widdrington. See *The Scots Magazine*, vol. III (Edinburgh, 1741), p. 382; Edwards, *Natural History of Uncommon Birds*, p. 209.

20 Theodorus Netscher, *Pineapple Grown in Sir Matthew Decker's Garden at Richmond, Surrey*, https://artuk.org, accessed 20 February 2018.

21 John Macky, *A Journey Through England: In Familiar Letters from a Gentleman Here to a Friend Abroad*, vol. I (London, 1722–3), p. 67. See also 'Pembroke Villa', www.richmond.gov.uk, accessed 20 February 2018.

22 James Bond, 'The Increase of those Creatures that are Bred and Fed in the Water Fishponds in England and Wales', in *Historical Aquaculture in Northern Europe*, ed. Madeleine Bonow, Håkan Olsén and Ingvar Svanberg (Huddinge, 2016), p. 188.

23 H. B. Morse, *Britain and the China Trade, 1635–1834*, vol. I (Oxford, 1926), pp. 230–31, *London Evening Post*, issue 1733 (21–3 December); *London Daily Journal*, issue 3947 (20 March 1732); Doreen Skala, 'Scarth Family Case Study: Jonathan Scarth the Younger', http://blogs.ucl.ac.uk/eicah, July 2014.

24 *London Daily Gazette*, issue 1146 (22 February 1739); Skala, 'Scarth Family Case Study'.

25 Morse, *Britain and the China Trade*, vol. I, p. 276. See Skala, 'Scarth Family Case Study'.

26 *Records of Fort St George, Letters from Fort St George, 1740*, vol. XXIV (Madras, 1932), p. 52; *London General Evening Post*, issue 1059 (5–8 July); *London Common Sense, or the Englishman's Journal*, issue 179 (13 July 1740). See Skala, 'Scarth Family Case Study'.

27 Edwards, *Natural History of Uncommon Birds*, p. 209.

28 Ibid.

29 Timothy J. McCann, *The Correspondence of The Dukes of Richmond and Newcastle, 1724–1750* (Lewes, 1982–3), p. xxix.

30 Charles Lennox to Martin Folkes, 12 November 1732, MS/865/11, Royal Society Library, London.

31 Charles Lennox to Martin Folkes, 26 November 1742, MS/865/11, Royal Society Library, London.

32 Goodwood MS/134, West Sussex Record Office, as quoted in McCann, *The Correspondence of The Dukes of Richmond and Newcastle*, p. xxix.

33 Henry Foster to Charles Lennox, 8 April 1730, Goodwood MS/108/815, West Sussex Record Office, as quoted in McCann, *The Correspondence of The Dukes of Richmond and Newcastle,* p. xxix.

34 George Edwards, *Gleanings of Natural History, Part II* (London, 1760), p. 210.

35 Thomas Pennant, *British Zoology*, vol. III (London, 1776), p. 327.

36 Bond, 'The Increase of those Creatures', p. 187.

37 David Porter, *The Chinese Taste in Eighteenth-century England* (Cambridge, 2010), pp. 20–21.

38 Ibid., p. 21.

39 Horace Walpole, *The Letters of Horace Walpole, Earl of Orford, 1744–1753*, vol. II (London, 1840), p. 344.

40 George F. Hervey and Jack Hems, *The Goldfish* (London, 1981), p. 80.

41 Walpole, *The Letters of Horace Walpole*, vol. II, pp. 80, 189 and 215.

42 Ibid., p. 251.

43 Hervey and Hems, *The Goldfish*, p. 82.

44 Walpole, *The Letters of Horace Walpole*, vol. II, p. 425.

45 Allison Meier, '18th-century Odes to a Cat that Drowned in a Goldfish Bowl', https://hyperallergic.com, 7 April 2016.

46 Anna Seward, 'An Old Cat's Dying Soliloquy', in *The Poetical Register, and Repository of Fugitive Poetry for 1803* (London, 1804), pp. 425–6.

47 'Joshua Reynolds: The Creation of Celebrity, Room 7, Kitty Fisher', www.tate.org.uk, September 2005.

48 'Kitty Fisher', www.npg.org.uk, accessed 25 February 2018.

49 'The Property of the Trustees of the Bowood Collection: Sir Joshua Reynolds, Portrait of Kitty Fisher', www.sothebys.com, 22 November 2007.

50 Gilbert White, *The Natural History and Antiquities of Selborne* (London, 1900), pp. 228–9.

51 [*qui variare cupit rem prodigialiter unam, delphinum silvis adpingit, fluctibus aprum: in vitium ducit culpae fuga, si caret arte.*]

52 Job Baster, *Natuurkundige Uitspanningen* (Haarlem, 1762).

53 Job Baster, 'A Dissertation on the Worms which destroy the Piles on the Coasts of Holland and Zealand', *Philosophical Transactions of the Royal Society*, XLI/455 (1739), pp. 276–88. See also Marc Ratcliff, *The Quest for the Invisible: Microscopy in the Enlightenment* (New York, 2016), p. 117.

54 Earl of March, *A Duke and his Friends: The Life and Letters of the Second Duke of Richmond* (London, 1911), pp. 138–9. See also MacGregor, 'Patrons and Collectors', p. 43, endnote 23.

55 Freddy van Nieulande, 'Het buffet van Baster', *Zeeland Magazine* (*Tijdschrift Zeeland*), XXIV/3 (July 2015), p. 108.

56 Job Baster to Carl Linnaeus, 29 November 1751, 1 April 1752, 1 September 1763, http://linnaeus.c18.net.

57 Van Nieulande, 'Het buffet van Baster', p. 109.

58 'Monticello Research Report, August 2003', www.monticello.org, accessed 28 February 2018.

59 Jan Hogendorn and Marion Johnson, *The Shell Money of the Slave Trade* (Cambridge, 2003), p. 46.

60 Van Nieulande, 'Het buffet van Baster', p. 109.

61 Albert Van Helden, *The Invention of the Telescope* (Philadelphia, PA, 1977).

62 David M. Damkaer, *The Copepodologist's Cabinet: A Biographical and Bibliographical History*, part 1 (Philadelphia, PA, 2002), pp. 59–60.

63 Baster, *Natuurkundige Uitspanningen*, pp. 86–7 [*Hier in Holland zyn dezelve, zoo als ik meen, reeds gebragt in de Jaaren 1753 of 1754, en wel het eerst op de Vyvers van Zorg-vlied en Hortekamp, Buitenplaatsen van den Wel Ed. Geb. Heer van Rhoon, en den Heer Clifford; doch zonder tot heden zoo my onderregt is, daar voortgeteeld te zyn*].

64 Ibid., p. 87 [*In de Maand November van het jaar 1758, kreeg ik voor het eerst twaalf van deze Visjes uit Engeland; it zette 'er agt van in ééne en vier op een andere Vyver van myn Tuin*].

65 Ibid., p. 86 [*De anderen veranderen trapsgewijs tot goud of zilver, met zodanige schitterenden luister, dat ons best verguldsel daar neit by kan haalen*].

66 Ibid., p. 91.

67 Job Baster to Carl Linnaeus, http://linnaeus.c18.net, 1 September 1763.

68 Daniel Defoe, 'Letter 7, Part 2: Cheshire and North-west Midlands', in *A Tour thro' the whole island of Great Britain, divided into circuits or journies* [1727] (Adelaide, 2014).

69 Alwyne C. Wheeler, 'The Gronovius Fish Collection: A Catalogue and Historical Account', *Bulletin of the British Museum* (Natural History), I/5 (1958), pp. 189–249, p. 212. The elder Gronovius incidentally edited the ninth edition of Linnaeus's famous work on taxonomy, the *Systema Naturae*. The Gronovius collection of plants and fish skins was bought at auction by John Stuart, Third Earl of Bute, who subsequently brought them to England. Joseph Banks bought the herbarium; the fish skins disappeared for a time and were bought at auction by the Natural History Museum. For the fish skin preservation method, see John Frederic Gronovius, 'A Method of Preparing Specimens of Fish, by Drying their Skins', *Philosophical Transactions of the Royal Society*, XLII/463 (1742–3), pp. 57–8.

70 Bond, 'The Increase of those Creatures', p. 14.

71 Ibid., p. 15.

72 'Instruktion till Magister Tärnström', in Carl Linnaeus, *Bref och skrifvelser af och till Carl von Linné. Utgifna och med upplysande noter försedda*, ed. T. M. Fries, J. M. Hulth and A. H. Uggla (Stockholm, 1907–43), part 1/2, pp. 53–4.

73 Pehr af Bjerkén to Carl Linnaeus, http://linnaeus.c18.net, 14 June 1758.

74 Mel Greaves, *Cancer: The Evolutionary Legacy* (Oxford, 2001), p. 14. See also Marjo Kaartinen, *Breast Cancer in the Eighteenth Century* (New York, 2015), pp. 9–10.

75 Richard Guy, *Practical Observations on Cancers and Disorders of the Breast* (London, 1762), p. 113.

76 Pehr af Bjerkén to Carl Linnaeus, http://linnaeus.c18.net,
     7 October 1759.
77 Ibid., 31 December 1760.

4 GOLDFISH BY THE MILLION AND THE AGE OF CONSUMERISM

 1 This point has been made about goldfish in American culture
     by Katherine C. Grier, 'Buying Your Friends: The Pet Business
     and American Consumer Culture', in *Commodifying Everything:
     Relationships of the Market*, ed. Susan Strasser (New York, 2003),
     pp. 43–70.
 2 Tim Birkhead, *The Red Canary: The Story of the First Genetically
     Engineered Animal* (London, 2004), p. 38.
 3 Ibid., p. 39.
 4 Henry Mayhew, *London Labour and the London Poor*, vol. II
     (London, 1865), p. 90. See also Mimi Matthews, 'A Brief History
     of Victorian Goldfish Globes and Goldfish-hawkers',
     www.mimimatthews.com, 9 June 2016.
 5 Mayhew, *London Labour and the London Poor*, vol. II, p. 90.
 6 Gilbert White, *The Natural History and Antiquities of Selborne*
     (London, 1900), pp. 228–9.
 7 Mayhew, *London Labour and the London Poor*, vol. I, p. 208; vol. II,
     p. 90.
 8 Ibid., vol. II, p. 92.
 9 Christopher Wood, *Victorian Painting* (London, 1999), p. 65.
10 Hasia Diner, 'German Jews and Peddling in America',
     in *Immigrant Entrepreneurship: German-American Business
     Biographies, 1720 to the Present*, ed. William J. Hausman,
     www.immigrantentrepreneurship.org, accessed 2 March 2018.
11 A dictionary technique also used by Katrina Gulliver, 'The Great
     Goldfish Invasion: How an Exotic Carp Took Over America',
     www.theatlantic.com, November 2012.
12 Noah Webster, *A Compendious Dictionary of the English Language:
     A Facsimile of the First (1806) Edition*, ed. Philip B. Gove
     (New York, 1970), p. 6.

13 Daniel Ammen, *Country Homes and Their Improvement* (Washington, DC, 1885), p. 4.

14 'Raising Fancy Goldfish', *New York Sun* (24 September 1911), p. 3.

15 'No More Free Goldfish', *Alexandria Gazette and Virginia Advertiser* (23 November 1894), p. 1. See also Gulliver, 'The Great Goldfish Invasion'.

16 'No More Free Goldfish'.

17 'The Public's Goldfish', *Evening Star*, 20 July 1912, part 1, p. 11.

18 'Why Goldfish Died in FDR Fountain', *Memphis World*, 30 May 1964, p. 6.

19 'The Winona History Center, Bill Sunday Home Museum', www.winonahistorycenter.com, accessed 6 March 2018.

20 W. A. Firstenberger, *In Rare Form: A Pictorial History of Baseball Evangelist Billy Sunday* (Iowa City, IA, 2005). My thanks to Rhoda Palmer of the Morgan Library, Grace College and Seminary for this information and for permission to use the postcard image.

21 My thanks to Keith Moore.

22 *Godey's Lady's Book*, ed. Sarah J. Hale and Louis A. Godey, vol. L (Philadelphia, PA, 1859), p. 119. This point was made by Katherine C. Grier, *Pets in America: A History* (Chapel Hill, NC, 2006), p. 52. *Godey's Lady's Book* seemed in their observations to have been inspired by Gilbert White, the eighteenth-century naturalist, who in 1781 noted much the same thing in a letter to Daines Barrington.

23 Derek B. Scott, *The Singing Bourgeois: Songs of the Victorian Drawing Room and Parlo* (Aldershot, 2001).

24 'Obituary Mary B. Hazelton', *The Townsman* (17 September 1953), p. 11.

25 Scott, *The Singing Bourgeois*.

26 Kurt Gänzl, 'The Geisha', in *The Encyclopedia of the Musical Theater*, http://operetta-research-center.org, accessed 5 March 2018.

27 Professor Faraday, 'The Chemical History of a Candle, Lecture VI, Conclusion', *Scientific American*, IV/17 (27 April 1861), p. 258.

28 Gulliver, 'The Great Goldfish Invasion'.

29 T. O'Conor Sloane, 'Centrifugal Force', *Scientific American*, LV/6 (7 August 1886), p. 89.

30 'Such is Life', *Arizona Republican* (10 November 1910), p. 2.

31 'Goldfish Bowls as Displayed in the Shops', *New York Tribune* (19 March 1915), p. 7.

32 J. E. Taylor, *The Aquarium: Its Inhabitants, Structure, and Management* (Edinburgh, 1910), p. 13.

33 Tim Wijgerde, 'Victorian Pioneers of the Marine Aquarium', www.advancedaquarist.com, February 2016.

34 Anna Thynne, 'On the Increase of Madrepores', *Annals and Magazine of Natural History*, III/18 (1859), p. 450.

35 Wijgerde, 'Victorian Pioneers'.

36 Silvia Granata, '"Let us hasten to the beach": Victorian Tourism and Seaside Collecting', *Lit: Literature Interpretation Theory*, XXVII/2 (2016), p. 98.

37 Ibid.

38 Philip Henry Gosse, *The Aquarium: An Unveiling of the Wonders of the Deep Sea* (London, 1854), p. 9.

39 Robert Warington, 'Notice of Observations on the Adjustment of the Relations between the Animal and Vegetable Kingdoms, by which the Vital Functions of Both are Permanently Maintained', *Journal of the Chemical Society*, III/1 (1851), pp. 52–4. See also Grier, *Pets in America*, p. 53; Christopher Hamlin, 'Robert Warington and the Moral Economy of the Aquarium', *Journal of the History of Biology*, XIX/1 (Spring 1986), p. 131.

40 Hamlin, 'Robert Warington', pp. 134–5.

41 Gosse, *The Aquarium*, p. 10.

42 Ibid., p. 250.

43 For an extended treatment of Gosse and the aquarium, see Bernd Brunner, *The Ocean at Home: An Illustrated History of the Aquarium* (London, 2005). See also Granata, 'Let us hasten', p. 104.

44 Gosse, *The Aquarium*, p. 164.

45 Henry Nicholls, 'Review of Bernd Brunner's *Ocean at Home*', *History Today*, www.historytoday.com, 6 June 2012.

46 'Combined Portable Aquarium and Wardian Case', *Scientific American*, XXXIII/7 (14 August 1875), p. 103.

47 Taylor, *The Aquarium*, p. 39.
48 Gosse, *The Aquarium*, pp. 250–52.
49 Ibid., p. 255.
50 Grace Wood and Emily Burbank, *The Art of Interior Decoration* (New York, 1919), pp. 105–6.
51 'Goldfish Bowls as Displayed in the Shops', *New York Tribune* (19 March 1915), p. 7.
52 P. White, *Poiret* (London, 1973), p. 7.
53 'Haute Couture's Grand Showman', www.studiointernational.com, accessed 5 March 2018; H. Koda and A. Bolton, *Poiret* (New York, 2007), p. 55.
54 'Goldfish Bowls as Displayed in the Shops', p. 7.
55 Henry G. Abbott, *The Watch Factories of America Past and Present* (Chicago, IL, 1888), p. 34.
56 'Art Deco Japanese Fishbowl', www.decophobia.com, accessed 9 March 2018.
57 Grier, *Pets in America*, p. 55.
58 William T. Innes, *The Complete Aquarium Book: The Care and Breeding of Goldfish and Tropical Fishes,* reprint (New York, 1936), p. 1.
59 Ibid., p. 10.
60 Ibid., p. 9.
61 Brunner, *The Ocean at Home*, p. 65.
62 'Raising Fancy Goldfish: A Kind of Backyard Farming that Yields Large Returns', *New York Sun* (24 September 1911), p. 3.
63 Ibid.
64 'Number 24. Golden Carp & Goldfish', Home Pets Series of 25, Issued by Godfrey Phillips Ltd, 112 Commercial St London', NYPL catalogue ID (B-number): b15262620, https://digitalcollections.nypl.org, accessed 1 July 2018.
65 Innes, *The Complete Aquarium Book*, p. 40.
66 'Raising Goldfish by the Million', *Popular Science* (September 1934), p. 108.
67 Betty Lee, *Marie Dressler, The Unlikeliest Star* (Lexington, KY, 2013), p. 127.

68 Max Alvarez, 'Cinema as an Imperialist Weapon: Hollywood and World War I', www.wsws.org, 5 August 2010.

69 Myron Stearns, 'Tropical Fish!', *Boy's Life* (February 1933), p. 13.

70 Hugh M. Smith, 'Goldfish and Their Cultivation in America', *National Geographic*, XLVI/4 (1924), p. 383. This is also a statistic cited in Grier, 'Buying Your Friends', p. 53.

71 'Raising Goldfish by the Million', *Popular Science* (September 1934), p. 26.

72 'Indiana has the Largest Gold Fish Farm in the World at Waldron', *Indianapolis News* (24 May 1902), p. 15.

73 Ibid.

74 Grier, 'Buying Your Friends', p. 53.

75 Robert R. Stickney, ed., *Culture of Nonsalmonid Freshwater Fishes*, 2nd edn (Boca Raton, FL, 1992), pp. 308 and 311.

76 'Advertisement, Kramer's Departmental Flower Stores', *Sunday Star* (8 January 1922), p. 21.

77 'Raising Goldfish by the Million', *Popular Science*, p. 24.

78 F. J. Bertuch, *Bilderbuch für Kinder* (Weimar, 1798), preface.

79 'Gold-fish', in *Harper's Young People: An Illustrated Weekly*, 1/6 (9 December 1879), p. 44.

80 'Goldfish Boiled', *Memphis World*, XXV/37 (28 November 1956), p. 4.

81 'Ford Motor Company Advertisement', 1964, J. Walter Thompson Company, Domestic Advertisements Collection, David M. Rubenstein Rare Book and Manuscript Library, Duke University, https://repository.duke.edu, accessed 24 March 2018.

82 Josie Ensor, 'Schoolgirl's Petition to ban Goldfish Prizes at Fairgrounds Gathers Support from MPs', *Daily Telegraph* (6 April 2013), www.telegraph.co.uk.

83 Geoff Herbert, 'NYS Fair 2014: Why Can't You Win Goldfish Prizes on the Midway Anymore?', www.syracuse.com, 27 August 2014.

84 'Council Bans Goldfish Bowls', www.abc.net.au, 24 July 2004.

85 'How to Keep that Goldfish from the Fair or the Festival Alive', www.nola.com, 9 June 2011.

86 Alison Spiegel, 'Goldfish are Apparently Soup Crackers', *Huffington Post* (11 December 2014), www.huffingtonpost.co.uk.

87 Doug Battema, 'Pepperidge Farm, Inc', in *The Advertising Age Encyclopedia of Advertising*, ed. John McDonough and Karen Egolf (New York, 2015), p. 1196.

88 Ibid.

89 JChaseFilms, 'We Won the Goldfish Stop-motion Contest!', www.youtube.com, accessed 19 March 2018.

5 GOLDFISH: VILLAIN AND HERO

1 Gene S. Helfman, *Fish Conservation: A Guide to Understanding and Restoring Global Aquatic Biodiversity and Fishery Resources* (Washington, DC, 2007), p. 220. See also Steph Yin, 'In the Wild, Goldfish Turn from Pet to Pest', www.nytimes.com, 22 September 2016.

2 Helfman, *Fish Conservation*, p. 220.

3 'List of Aquatic Nuisance Species in other States, January 2016, Colorado Parks and Wildlife', http://cpw.state.co.us, accessed 20 March 2018.

4 Charlie Brennan, 'Boulder Goldfish Go Global – but Eradication Plan Not Finalised', www.dailycamera.com, 10 April 2015.

5 'Invasive Goldfish Dumped at Teller Lake #5 in Boulder', http://cpw.state.co.us, 6 April 2015.

6 Charlie Brennan, 'Hungry Pelicans Credited with Gobbling Thousands of Goldfish infesting Boulder Lake', www.dailycamera.com, 28 April 2015.

7 'Aquatic Wildlife Management: Draft Regulation Informational Packet, Marked Regulation Changes', http://cpw.state.co.us, 26 September 2017.

8 Brian Clark Howard, '"Monster" Goldfish Multiplying in Lake Tahoe: Freshwater Species of the Week', https://blog. nationalgeographic.org, 21 February 2013.

9 S. J. Beatty et al., 'First Evidence of Spawning Migration by Goldfish (*Carassius auratus*); Implications for Control of a Globally Invasive Species', *Ecology of Freshwater Fish*, XXVI/3 (2017), pp. 444–55.

10 Ewen Callaway, 'Evolutionary Biology: The Lost Appetites', *Nature*, 486 (21 June 2012), pp. s16–s17.

11 Paul S. Pittenger and Charles E. Vanderkleed, 'Preliminary Note on a New Pharmacodynamic Assay Method', *Journal of the American Pharmaceutical Association*, IV/4 (1915), pp. 427–33.

12 William Withering, 'An Account of the Foxglove, and Some of its Medical Uses', in *The Miscellaneous Tracts . . . of William Withering*, vol. I (London, 1822), p. 113.

13 Ibid., p. 122.

14 Paul S. Pittenger, 'Preliminary Note on a New Pharmacodynamic Assay Method (Continuation of a Previously Reported Paper)', *Journal of the American Pharmaceutical Association,* VIII/11 (1919), p. 893.

15 Ibid.

16 Ralph S. Ryback, 'Effect of Ethanol, Bourbon and Various Ethanol Levels on Y-maze Learning in the Goldfish', *Psychopharmacologia*, XIV/4 (1969), p. 306.

17 F. Damrau and E. Liddy, 'The Whiskey Congeners: Comparison of Whiskey with Vodka as to Toxic Effects', *Current Therapeutic Research*, II (1960), pp. 453–7.

18 Catherine. E. Fagernes et al., 'Extreme Anoxia Tolerance in Crucian Carp and Goldfish through Neofunctionalization of Duplicated Genes creating a new Ethanol-producing Pyruvate Decarboxylase Pathway', *Scientific Reports*, VII/1 (2017), p. 7884.

19 Avril D. Woodhead, *Nonmammalian Animal Models for Biomedical Research* (Boca Raton, FL, 1989), p. 227.

20 Philip Gee, David Stephenson and Donald E. Wright, 'Temporal Discrimination Learning of Operant Feeding in Goldfish (*Carassius auratus*)', *Journal of the Experimental Analysis of Behavior*, LXII/1 (1994), pp. 1–13.

21 'Zoology: How Sounds Make Goldfish Skittish', *Nature*, 478 (6 October 2011), p. 9.

22 Andrew R. Cossins, 'A Warm Topic for Cognition, Review of "The Hot Brain: Survival, Temperature, and the Human Body"',

Nature, 407 (19 October 2000), p. 837.

23 'Man Trains Goldfish to Go Through Hoops, Push Soccer Ball';
'Fish Can Quickly Learn Complex Tricks', www.underwatertimes.
com, 16 December 2005; 'Professor Trains Goldfish to Recognise
Objects', www.underwatertimes.com, 28 October 2011. For a video
of Poseidon in action, see www.youtube.com.

24 C. M. DeLong et al., 'Small and Large Number Discrimination in
Goldfish (*Carassius auratus*) with Extensive Training', *Behavioural
Processes*, cxli/2 (24 November 2016), pp. 172–83.

25 Robert Chandler, 'Alexander Pushkin: A Tale About a Fisherman
and a Fish', www.stosvet.net, accessed 20 March 2018.

Select Bibliography

Ammen, Daniel, *Country Homes and Their Improvement* (Washington, DC, 1885)

Balon, E. K., 'About the Oldest Domesticates Among Fishes', *Journal of Fish Biology*, 65 (2004), pp. 1–27

Baster, Job, *Natuurkundige Uitspanningen* (Haarlem, 1762)

Beatty, S. J. et al., 'First Evidence of Spawning Migration by Goldfish (*Carassius auratus*); Implications for Control of a Globally Invasive Species', *Ecology of Freshwater Fish*, 26 (2017), pp. 444–55

Bertuch, F. J., *Bilderbuch für Kinder* (Weimar, 1798)

Billardon de Sauvigny, Edme-Louis, *Histoire naturelle des dorades de la Chine* (Paris, 1780)

Birkhead, Tim, *The Red Canary: The Story of the First Genetically Engineered Animal* (London, 2004)

Bloch, Marcus, *Ichthyologie; ou, histoire naturelle des poissons. En six parties avec 216 planches dessinées et enluminées d'après nature*, 6 vols (Berlin, 1796)

Bond, James, 'The Increase of those Creatures that are Bred and Fed in the Water Fishponds in England and Wales', in *Historical Aquaculture in Northern Europe*, ed. Madeleine Bonow, Håkan Olsén and Ingvar Svanberg (Huddinge, 2016), pp. 157–99

Brunner, Bernd, *The Ocean at Home: An Illustrated History of the Aquarium* (London, 2005)

Chen, Shisan C., 'A History of the Domestication and the Factors of the Varietal Formation of the Common Goldfish, *Carassius Auratus*', *Scientia Sinica*, V/1–4 (1956), pp. 287–321

Edwards, George, *Natural History of Uncommon Birds and of Some Other Rare and Undescribed Animals* (London, 1743–51)

Firstenberger, W. A., *In Rare Form: A Pictorial History of Baseball Evangelist Billy Sunday* (Iowa City, IA, 2005)

Gee, Philip, David Stephenson and Donald E. Wright, 'Temporal Discrimination Learning of Operant Feeding in Goldfish (*Carassius auratus*)', *Journal of the Experimental Analysis of Behaviour*, 62 (1994), pp. 1–13

Goldgar, Anne, *Impolite Learning: Conduct and Community in the Republic of Letters, 1680–1750* (New Haven, CT, 1995)

Gosse, Philip Henry, *The Aquarium: An Unveiling of the Wonders of the Deep Sea* (London, 1854)

Granata, Silvia, '"Let us hasten to the beach": Victorian Tourism and Seaside Collecting', *Lit: Literature Interpretation Theory*, XXVII/2 (2016), pp. 91–110

Grier, Katherine C., 'Buying Your Friends: The Pet Business and American Consumer Culture', in *Commodifying Everything: Relationships of the Market*, ed. Susan Strasser (New York, 2003), pp. 43–70

—, *Pets in America: A History* (Chapel Hill, NC, 2006)

Grigson, Caroline, *Menagerie: The History of Exotic Animals in England, 1100–1837* (Oxford, 2016)

Gulliver, Katrina, 'The Great Goldfish Invasion: How an Exotic Carp Took Over America', www.theatlantic.com, 1 November 2012

Hamlin, Christopher, 'Robert Warington and the Moral Economy of the Aquarium', *Journal of the History of Biology*, XIX/1 (Spring 1986), pp. 131–53

Helfman, Gene S., *Fish Conservation: A Guide to Understanding and Restoring Global Aquatic Biodiversity and Fishery Resources* (Washington, DC, 2007)

Hervey, George F., and Jack Hems, *The Goldfish* (London, 1981)

Innes, William T., *The Complete Aquarium Book: The Care and Breeding of Goldfish and Tropical Fishes* (New York, 1936)

Koda, H., and A. Bolton, *Poiret* (New York, 2007)

McDonough, John, and Karen Egolf, eds, *The Advertising Age Encyclopedia of Advertising* (New York, 2015)

MacGregor, Arthur, 'Patrons and Collectors: Contributors of Zoological Subjects to the Works of George Edwards (1694–1773)', *Journal of the History of Collections*, xxvi/1 (1 March 2014), pp. 35–44

Mayhew, Henry, *London Labour and the London Poor* (London, 1865)

Morse, H. B., *Britain and the China Trade, 1635–1834*, vol. i: *The Chronicles of the East India Company Trading to China* (Oxford, 1926)

Mulertt, Hugo, *The Goldfish and its Systemic Culture* (New York, 1910)

Petiver, James, *Gazophylacium Naturae et Artis*, in *Opuscula Petiveriana* (London, 1695–1717)

Pittenger, Paul S., and Charles E. Vanderkleed, 'Preliminary Note on a New Pharmacodynamic Assay Method', *Journal of the American Pharmaceutical Association*, iv/4 (1915), pp. 427–33

Porter, David, *The Chinese Taste in Eighteenth-century England* (Cambridge, 2010)

Ryback, Ralph S., 'Effect of Ethanol, Bourbon and Various Ethanol Levels on Y-maze Learning in the Goldfish', *Psychopharmacologia*, xiv/4 (1969), pp. 305–14

Smartt, Joseph, *Goldfish Varieties and Genetics: A Handbook for Breeders* (Oxford, 2008)

Stickney, Robert R., ed., *Culture of Nonsalmonid Freshwater Fishes*, 2nd edn (Boca Raton, FL, 1992)

Takaoka, Kazuya, and Sachiko Kuru, *Kingyo: The Artistry of Japanese Goldfish* (Tokyo, New York and London, 2003)

Taylor, J. E., *The Aquarium: Its Inhabitants, Structure, and Management* (Edinburgh, 1910)

Thynne, Anna, 'On the Increase of Madrepores', *Annals and Magazine of Natural History*, iii/18 (1859), pp. 449–61

Warington, Robert, 'Notice of Observations on the Adjustment of the Relations between the Animal and Vegetable Kingdoms, by which the Vital Functions of Both are Permanently Maintained', *Journal of the Chemical Society*, iii/1 (1851), pp. 52–4

Wheeler, Alwyne C., 'The Gronovius Fish Collection: A Catalogue
    and Historical Account', *Bulletin of the British Museum* (Natural
    History), 1/5 (1958), pp. 189–249
White, Gilbert, *The Natural History and Antiquities of Selborne*
    (London, 1900)
Wood, Christopher, *Victorian Painting* (London, 1999)

Associations and Websites

L'ASSOCIATION FRANÇAISE DU POISSON ROUGE
www.lepoissonrouge.org
For French goldfish keepers, with very good videos of varieties.

THE ASSOCIATION OF MIDLAND GOLDFISH KEEPERS
http://amgk.co.uk
Meeting near Coventry, and dedicated to the care and keeping of fancy goldfish.

BRISTOL AQUARISTS' SOCIETY
www.bristol-aquarists.org.uk
Founded in 1929, the Society's aims are to 'advance the study and enjoyment of goldfish and all coldwater life', and to 'keep and breed the various strains of fancy goldfish, and to exhibit them at shows'. A valuable resource to understand goldfish varieties and aquaculture.

FISH LINK CENTRAL
www.fishlinkcentral.com
List of aquarium resources on the Internet.

GOLDFISH KEEPERS
www.goldfishkeepers.com
Noteworthy for its active forum announcing competitions and informative articles.

GOLDFISH SOCIETY OF AMERICA
www.goldfishsociety.org
While this national society is dedicated primarily to goldfish, they also
serve many water gardeners and koi enthusiasts.

GOLDFISH SOCIETY OF GREAT BRITAIN
http://gsgb.co.uk
Founded in 1948, and the largest goldfish club in Britain.

THE GOLDFISH TANK
http://thegoldfishtank.com
Excellent hobbyist site devoted to the care and feeding of goldfish.

THE INTERNATIONAL FEDERATION OF ONLINE CLUBS AND AQUATIC
SOCIETIES
www.ifocas.org
List and links to fish clubs of the world.

KORIYAMA GOLDFISH MUSEUM
www.kingyoen.com
The goldfish museum mecca, exhibiting forty types of goldfish.

LINNAEAN CORRESPONDENCE
http://linnaeus.c18.net
Sponsored by the Royal Swedish Academy of Sciences, Uppsala University and its library, and the Linnaean Society of London, with the
collaboration of the Centre international d'étude du XVIIIe siècle, this
site has scans of Carl Linnaeus's letters and editions of this work.
Excellent for those interested in the history of natural history.

THE LONDON AQUARIUM
www.visitsealife.com/london
Mostly marine life, but freshwater species are also on exhibit.

NATURAL HISTORY MUSEUM, LONDON ZOOLOGY COLLECTIONS
www.nhm.ac.uk/our-science/collections/zoology-collections.html
29 million animal specimens available to search.

OOZEKI RANCHU CLUB OF SINGAPORE
www.oozekiranchuclub.com/
A hobbyist's club founded in 2000 to promote the interest of rearing
Japanese Ranchu though study, research and exhibitions.

SOLID GOLD AQUATICS YOUTUBE CHANNEL
www.youtube.com/user/flashofpink
Created by Jennifer Lynx, a tremendous resource on goldfish care and
varieties.

THE VERMILLION GOLDFISH CLUB
http://vermilliongoldfishclub.com
The first goldfish club of Singapore. In Chinese and English, with an
excellent blog by a goldfish judge featuring fish care and goldfish art.

Acknowledgements

This book was one of those inspired by staring out of the train window, my brain empty, until I imagined goldfish swimming in and out of my ears. Conversations with Ian Benton, Yupin Chung, Keith Moore and Charlotte Sleigh helped too. Several librarians and libraries including the Bodleian Library, British Library, Cambridge University Library, Grace College and Seminary, the Huntington and the Royal Society Library filled in the details. My thanks to Brian van Geer and his family for giving me a tour of Job Baster's house. Jonathan Burt, the acquisitions editor for Reaktion, was consistently delightful. Thanks to all, and special thanks (and apologies) to Speedy, my first pet goldfish.

Photo Acknowledgements

The author and publishers wish to express their thanks to the below sources of illustrative material and/or permission to reproduce it. Some locations of artworks are also given below, in the interests of brevity:

Eamon Ambrose/Freeimages.com: p. 17; from Job Baster, *Opuscula subseciva, observations miscellaneas de animalculis et plantis . . . Tom. II. Liber II* (Haarlem, 1765), © The Royal Society, London: p. 86; © Österreichische Galerie Belvedere, Vienna: pp. 107 (Inv.-Nr. 3708), 121 (Inv.-Nr. 1829); Glenn Bennett/Shutterstock.com: p. 151; from Friedrich Justin Bertuch, *Bilderbuch für Kinder*, vol. I, 2nd edn (Weimar and Gotha, 1801): p. 139; BlackRabbit3/Shutterstock.com: p. 45; from Marc Bloch, *Ichtyologie, ou, Histoire naturelle, generale et particuliere des poissons* (Berlin, 1785–97), vol. III–IV, photo Biodiversity Heritage Library: p. 8; Boston Public Library: p. 145; from *Cassell's Household Guide*, vol. III (London and New York, *c.* 1869), photo Old Design Shop: p. 116; from *Cat Tales: Interesting and Instructive Stories of our Favorite Household Pet* (Boston, MA, *c.* 1893), photo The University of Florida, George A. Smathers Libraries: p. 140; City of Edinburgh Council: p. 108; Cmoulton/Dreamstime.com: p. 144; collection of the author: pp. 37, 42, 128; © CSG CIC Glasgow Museums and Libraries Collections: p. 23; Peter Dakomd/Pixabay.com: p. 158; Decophobia 20th Century Design/Decophobia.com: p. 129; from Josef Maria Eder and Eduard Valenta, *Versuche über Photographie mittelst der Röntgen'schen Strahlen* (Vienna and Halle, 1896), photo The Metropolitan Museum of Art, New York: p. 12; from George Edwards, *A Natural History of Uncommon Birds and of Some Other Rare and Undescribed*

Animals, vol. IV (London, 1750), © The Royal Society, London: p. 70; from George Edwards, *Gleanings of Natural History*, vol. II (London, 1760), photo Biodiversity Heritage Library: p. 73; Finchfocus/Shutterstock.com: p. 62; from George Brown Goode, et al., *The Fisheries and Fishery Industries of the United States, Section 1: Natural History of Useful Aquatic Animals* (Washington, DC, 1884): p. 99; from Philip Henry Gosse, *The Aquarium: An Unveiling of the Wonders of the Deep Sea*, 2nd edn (London, 1856), photo Biodiversity Heritage Library: p. 122; from Ernest d'Hervilly and Gustave Fraipont, *Les Bêtes à Paris* (Paris, 1885), photo Bibliothèque nationale de France: p. 109; History and Art Collection/Alamy Stock Photo: p. 97; from Walter Houghton, *British Fresh-water Fishes*, vol. I (London, 1879), © The Royal Society, London: p. 105; Iliuta Goean/Dreamstime.com: p. 98; Indiana Historical Society: pp. 133, 134, 135 (P0408), 143 (P0178); from the *Indianapolis News* (24 May 1902), Hoosier State Chronicles: p. 136; from William T. Innes, *Goldfish Varieties and Tropical Aquarium Fishes* (Philadelphia, PA, *c.* 1917), photo Biodiversity Heritage Library: pp. 131, 132; Isselee/Dreamstime.com: p. 167; Mike Johnson/FreeImages.com: p. 146; from *Journal des Dames et des Modes, Costumes Parisiens*, no. 61 (1913), photo Rijksmuseum, Amsterdam (Open Access): p. 125; KPG Payless2/Shutterstock.com: p. 38; Library of Congress, Washington, DC: pp. 101, 102, 132, 142 (Prints and Photographs Division), 138 (Chronicling America), Lightzoom/Dreamstime.com: p. 51; Los Angeles County Museum of Art: p. 50; The Metropolitan Museum of Art, New York: pp. 28, 29, 36, 40, 43, 48, 49, 58, 130; from Koloman Moser, *Die Quelle: Flächen Schmuck* or *The Source: Ornament for Flat Surfaces* (Vienna, 1901): p. 124; National Archives at College Park, Maryland: p. 148; National Gallery of Victoria, Melbourne, Felton Bequest, 1939 (3924–D3): p. 30; © National Portrait Gallery, London: pp. 81, 110; from V. Nèlis, *Vertel eens wat!, Louwerse's kinderprenten*, series IV, no. 24 (Zutphen, 1905–24), photo Rijksmuseum, Amsterdam, Gift of F. G. Waller: p. 141; from The New York Public Library: pp. 41, 54, 96 (Irma and Paul Milstein Division of United States History, Local History and Genealogy), 111; Payless Images/Shutterstock.com: p. 46; from James Petiver, *Gazophylacium naturae et artis* (London, 1702), © The Royal Society, London: p. 65; from Aleksandr Sergeevich Pushkin, *Skazka o*

Readers are free:

to share – to copy and redistribute the material in any medium or format
to remix – to adapt this image alone

Under the following conditions:

attribution – You must attribute the work in the manner specified by the author or licensor (but not in any way that suggests that they endorse you or your use of the work).
NoDerivatives – If you remix, transform, or build upon the material, you may not distribute the modified material.
share alike – If you alter, transform, or build upon this work, you may distribute the resulting work only under the same or similar license to this one.

Index

Page numbers in *italics* refer to illustrations